The IEA Health and Welfare Unit

Choice in Welfare No. 35

KU-708-586

Zero Tolerance:
Policing a Free Society

William J. Bratton

Ray Mallon
John Orr
Charles Pollard

Norman Dennis (Editor)

IEA Health and Welfare Unit
London

First published April 1997

The IEA Health and Welfare Unit
2 Lord North St
London SW1P 3LB

© The IEA Health and Welfare Unit 1997

ISBN 0-255 36395-8
ISSN 1362-9565

Typeset by the IEA Health and Welfare Unit
in Bookman 10 point
Printed in Great Britain by
Hartington Fine Arts Ltd, Lancing, West Sussex

Contents

The Authors

William J. Bratton began his career as a police officer in Boston in 1970, rising by 1980 to the position of Superintendent of Police. He served as Chief of the Massachusetts Bay Transportation Authority Police and as Superintendent of the Metropolitan District Commission Police. Between 1990 and 1992 he achieved national recognition for his leadership of the New York City Transit Police, initiating reforms and strategies that eventually cut subway crime by nearly 50 per cent. In 1992 he returned to Boston as Superintendent-in-Chief, and became Boston Police Commissioner in 1993. In January 1994 he was appointed Police Commissioner of the City of New York by Mayor Rudolph Giuliani, and embarked on a major reformation of the New York Police Department. He is now Vice Chairman of the Boston-based First Security Services Corporation and President of its New York subsidiary First Security Consulting, Inc.

Norman Dennis is Guest Fellow in the Department of Religious Studies, at the University of Newcastle upon Tyne. With Professor A.H. Halsey he is author of *English Ethical Socialism*, Clarendon Press, 1988. The IEA Health and Welfare Unit is the publisher of his *Families Without Fatherhood* (co-author George Erdos), 1993 (second edition) and *The Invention of Permanent Poverty*, 1996. He is also well-known for his study of a Yorkshire coal-mining town, *Coal Is Our Life* (with Cliff Slaughter and Fernando Henriques), and his two studies of a working-class district of Sunderland, *People and Planning*, 1970, and *Public Participation and Planners' Blight*, 1972. He is currently studying the struggle between the bureaucratic, political and media advocates of drug, educational and family permissiveness in the European Union and Switzerland, and one of their most important opponents, a Zürich citizens' organization called the VPM.

Ray Mallon is a native of Stockton-on-Tees. He lives there with his wife and their two daughters (aged 15 and 13). He joined the Cleveland Constabulary in June 1974. He served as a foot patrol officer in his home town and as a traffic patrol officer at Billingham (again, locally) before transferring for a brief period to Merseyside Police in 1977. In 1978 he re-joined Cleveland

Constabulary, and served with the Regional Crime Squad. After a period with the Cadet Training Department he served with the CID at Langbaugh. He was then appointed to head crime strategy at Hartlepool. He is now head of crime at Middlesbrough.

John Orr OBE QPM CIMgt joined the Kilmarnock Burgh Police in 1964. In 1969 he joined the former Ayrshire Constabulary and in 1984 he was appointed Head of Strathclyde Police Serious Crime Squad. He was promoted Detective Chief Superintendent in 1987, becoming Joint Head of Strathclyde CID. He was chosen to head the investigation into the Lockerbie air disaster and subsequently lectured extensively on disaster planning and investigation. He was appointed Director of the Management of Disasters and Civil Emergency Course at the Police Staff College, Bramshill, in 1992 and 1993. In 1990 he was appointed Deputy Chief Constable of Dumfries and Galloway Constabulary and in 1994, on secondment, Assistant Inspector of Constabulary for Scotland. Mr Orr was appointed Chief Constable of Strathclyde Police in January 1996. He was awarded the OBE in 1992 and the Queen's Police Medal in 1996. Mr Orr is married with a grown-up family of two sons and a daughter.

Charles Pollard QPM LLB joined the Metropolitan Police in 1964. He attended the 9th Special Course at the Police Staff College, Bramshill in 1971 where he gained a scholarship to Bristol University and obtained an Honours Degree in Law. He then served a further five years with the Metropolitan Police, being closely involved in the Balcombe Street siege and the Iranian Embassy siege. In 1980 he was promoted Superintendent in the Sussex Police where he was involved in the police operation at the Brighton bomb incident during the 1984 Conservative Party Conference. He was promoted Assistant Chief Constable in the Thames Valley Police in 1985, then returned to the Metropolitan Police as Deputy Assistant Commissioner in 1988. He was subsequently appointed Chief Constable of Thames Valley Police in January 1991. He was awarded the Queen's Police Medal in 1990 and is a Visiting Fellow of Nuffield College, Oxford.

Foreword

Zero Tolerance: Policing a Free Society brings together police officers from both sides of the Atlantic to describe their efforts to deal effectively with rising crime. Anyone who visits or lives in New York is aware of the significant reduction in its crime rate following the introduction of 'zero-tolerance' policing under the leadership of William Bratton. In the first essay Mr Bratton describes the philosophy behind the NYPD's change of strategy.

At about the same time, a similar experiment was being conducted in Hartlepool under the leadership of Ray Mallon. The guiding philosophy and results are described in our third essay, co-authored by Ray Mallon and Norman Dennis. The blend of the sociologist's insights with the practical knowledge of a serving police officer committed to the tradition of British policing that is restrained, good-humoured and yet effective has produced an essay of rare quality.

We are also fortunate to have essays by ·two distinguished Chief Constables. John Orr writes of the four-month-old experiment in Strathclyde to tackle crime and disorder by means of its 'Spotlight Initiative'. There are differences between the zero tolerance of the NYPD and the new police tactics being pursued in Strathclyde, but there is also much common ground.

Charles Pollard's essay is the least sympathetic to zero-tolerance policing and warns of some inherent dangers. However, policing in Thames Valley has drawn on the 'broken-windows' philosophy elaborated by George Kelling and James Q. Wilson (see below p. 45) which argues that small signs of disorder in a locality, like broken windows or graffiti, can encourage more serious criminality by giving rise to a sense that nobody cares.

With the benefit of a masterly introduction by Norman Dennis the collection explores the dilemmas that lie at the heart of any free society. Liberty depends on law, but if the agents of enforcement stray outside proper limits, liberty itself is threatened. No less important, there can be no freedom if we are afraid to leave our homes for fear of break-in or to venture into some parts of our cities because we fear assault.

The authors have thrown new light on how we can improve police effectiveness without over-stepping the legal limits that guard our liberties.

David G. Green

Editor's Introduction

Norman Dennis

Zero-Tolerance Policing

THE TERM 'zero tolerance' is an unfortunate one. Few people, least of all those brought up in and professionally trained to respect British traditions, are in favour of intolerance, or would admit it if they were. Reacting only to the term, without knowing what it refers to, clergymen assume that it means lack of compassion (whereas it is compassion's necessary pre-condition); and defenders of a free society assume that it means the repression of civil liberties (whereas it is the only way to secure them).

'Zero tolerance' is the label for a form of policing that was introduced quite independently but at just about the same time in New York, under its mayor Rudolph Giuliani, and in Hartlepool under DCI Ray Mallon.

The essence of the badly-named zero-tolerance crime strategy is not intolerance but confidence. It is marked in the first place by the confidence of the police officer in handling situations that come within his lawful purview, down to the lowest level of sub-criminal, quality-of-life, offences.

Whether a quality-of-life offence is dealt with by a joke, or with the lightest of hands that is required by the situation, it is dealt with with a view to stopping the offence, and stopping a repetition of it. The objective that is to prevail is clear. It is the police officer's, not the culprit's. The tactics to achieve the objective will always be as tolerant as possible. But the tactics are those of the police officer, not those of the offender or his pressure-group protector.

It is confident policing in a second sense. Under such policing the public is confident that the police, decently and within laws strongly oriented towards the defence of civil liberties, are effectively protecting them from attacks on their right to go about their business without interference, not only from criminals, but from louts.

In the book I wrote some time ago with George Erdos, *Families Without Fatherhood*, we tell a story about zero-tolerance, confident, policing in Sunderland in 1941. Three boys were sharing a Woodbine one Sunday morning in the loading bay of a town-centre store. A policeman appeared at one end of the short back lane, another at the other. The boys were marched home to their parents. (The boys and the policemen both walked a mile.) Their fathers smoked. The policemen smoked. But boys of twelve were not allowed to smoke. They certainly could not thumb their noses at generalized adult authority by smoking in public. The boys whose fathers were not away fighting in the war were in trouble with their fathers. All of them were in trouble with their mothers.

If any journalist had seen fit to write an article condemning the waste of police resources on a trivial—and victimless—offence when their fathers and brothers were being killed at the front or at sea, his editor would have wondered what on earth his point could be. If the editor had published it, the public would have had difficulty in understanding what was being proposed—that because their fathers were absent, their sons should be allowed to flout rules that they would have upheld if they had been at home?

When policing was detailed and consensual, we conclude, it was low-key, good humoured, and effective.[1] Of these three boys from working-class homes in terrace houses without gardens and opening straight onto the street, the products of depression and war, one became one of the town's best ship-yard welders, one a bank manager, and one the head of a polytechnic.

They were brought up in a culture which reserved its honour for conduct that was exemplified at its highest by the Pilsley colliery deputy, Frank Nix, in 1944. In spite of having his own family to think of, as well as himself, with extraordinary bravery, skill and intelligence he saved the life of Ernest Vickers, a miner trapped under a coal-cutting machine when the coal-face collapsed, and was in imminent danger of collapsing again and killing them both. That was the sort of deed these three boys talked about three or four years after their Woodbine experience, and he is the sort of man they talk about today.[2]

Zero-tolerance policing is based on three ideas. One is the simple principle, 'nip things in the bud'. Prevent anti-social elements developing the feeling that they are in charge. Prevent a broken-down and ugly environment of neglect becoming a breeding ground for crime and disorder.

The second idea is that, in comparison with serious offences, *low-intensity, humane, good-natured* control—in those senses 'tolerant' control—of these smaller challenges to the give-and-take of decent social intercourse is a tactic open to the police officer.

The third follows from the first two. At this low level of control, zero-tolerance policing can make a distinct difference, directly by reducing petty crime, vandalism, graffiti and low-level disorder, and indirectly by creating an environment less hospitable to more serious criminals.

A handful of young people sleep in the shop doorways of the Strand, one of the thoroughfares most frequented by visitors as they move between the West End and the City. Those who sleep in the entrances of the theatres are even more likely to shock rich visitors staying at the Savoy. Several hundred are spread across other very public locations. They are a tremendous asset to people who want to revolutionize the economy and income distribution of the country. Because as long as they are there, this tangle of personal and social failure can be held up to the world as decisive living proof that 'the system' is all to blame, and that Britain's social and economic order is rotten to the core. Compassion and moral indignation on their behalf is abundant and genuine. But compassion is mitigated by the requirement that they or their replacements must not be involuntarily removed from these most public of public arenas. They are too valuable as radical propaganda for that. They are conspicuous proofs of the bankruptcy of state housing policy, state benefits policy and state social-services policy. It is called 'the propaganda of the deed'.

There is enormous compassion and concern in London and the provinces for the homeless, especially but by no means exclusively for the mentally ill and others where it is pretty clearly 'no fault of their own'. But whether they congregate unhindered at Kings Cross or in the Strand or not, whether the police ignore them or direct them to accommodation or treatment, does not affect the daily life of most people except in the compassionate sense. But very many people in London and the provinces are now concerned on a daily basis with the local burglars, the local vandals, the local graffiti artists, the local gangs of bullies on their own estates and in their own small neighbourhoods.

But it does not seem to matter to those who defend the right of the homeless to sleep with maximum public exposure in the doorways of the main public thoroughfares, or against the warm-air vents of hotels, that zero-tolerance policing outside central London is in practice concerned almost entirely with lowering the incidence of these *unproblematical and consensually defined* offences that ought to be stopped. These offences, against property, against the person and against the quality of life, affect everyone directly, day by day.

In the current discussion everything is focused, not simply on the difficult and diverse subject of 'homelessness', but on probably the smallest, and from the point of view of civil liberties the least problematical, part of the homelessness problem—people who beg politely and choose to sleep in a shop doorway in preference to a hostel.

The much simpler, straightforward and far more pervasive and widespread problems throughout the country, including central London, caused by petty crime, affecting infinitely more people, are shuffled out of the debate.

All that confident policing says is that, so far as it is a policing matter, boys and young men will be stopped from handling their problems in ways that are useless to themselves and unpleasant for decent, law-abiding citizens. If they smash bottles on the pavement, scrawl graffiti on house walls, tear apart the bus shelter, gather in intimidating groups at the shopping centre, then it will not be overlooked. What use is it to anybody to keep *those* ways open to them?

What does the Archbishop of Canterbury mean when he says that 'clamping down is not the way to solve the problem'?[3] Whoever said or thought it was? No police strategy by itself, no matter how effective, can return crime to the levels of forty years ago. There has been a profound displacement of perception and values, which has left the English population much more prone to react to problems in self-destructive and anti-social ways, with a decline in a culture of responsibility, a rise in a culture of victimhood, and a transfer of attributions of causality from the cultural to the material environment. That displacement is by no means unconnected with the change over the same period in the messages preached from British pulpits.[4]

Police forces can hardly touch the problem of the dismembered family. Too many messages are still being transmitted to boys and young men—and of course to the girls and women who might become the mothers of their children—that urge them all to give priority to their own individual objectives in their self-regarding way of life. Police forces can hardly touch the problem of motivating a boy or young man to maximize his potential at school and in the community. Police forces now operate in a cultural and media environment in which the essential distinction has been forgotten (or has never been made by the people concerned) between the role of judicially-imposed punishments in deterring the more-or-less committed and incorrigible culprit himself (where their deterrence value is comparatively weak) and their role in deterring an at-present law-abiding boy or young man (where their deterrence value is strong).

None of these things are to any significant extent within the scope or competence of police officers to change.

But it is completely misleading to insinuate into the discussion the logical *non sequitur* that, because a particular form of activity cannot change everything, it can change nothing; or because it may not be able to change things quickly, it is useless to try to change them at all.

Police officers have a very specific job to do. They are not and cannot be all-purpose social workers. So far as their legal powers and rules of guidance permit, and public opinion allows, it is to see that people can go about their lawful business within a public environment which has not been gratuitously degraded, in an atmosphere of reasonable give-and-take, and without great anxiety that their homes or cars will have been broken into when they return to them.

Not 'clamping down' on minor misdemeanours, if 'clamping down' is the question-begging phrase the Archbishop of Canterbury wants to use, is the certain way of *not* solving the problem. For not only do you not solve the problem in the form in which it becomes manifest to the public, and in so far as it is controllable by the police. You provide a breeding ground in which the same and worse problems can fester. 'Clamping down'—confident policing within its proper limited domain—does not pretend to be the whole solution to any problem. It is meant to remove the problem from a context where it *can't possibly* be solved, into a context where it *might* be solved.

The scope for compassionate treatment of the problems that underlie the mentally ill adrift in the city, the failures of the local-authority care systems, vandalism, sleeping out in the street, injecting heroin, living for the next drink, knocking an elderly cyclist off his bike for a laugh, smashing windows, dropping bricks and bits of concrete from the bridge onto motorists passing underneath, looting empty houses,[5] is not restricted in the slightest if the police do *their* job confidently, with the public putting their confidence in what they are doing.

As Charles Pollard shows in this volume, shared assumptions about crime can lead to a variety of policing strategies. 'Neighbourhood policing' in San Diego is not the same as 'zero-tolerance policing' in New York City. 'Confident policing' in Hartlepool is not identical with 'problem-solving policing' in the Thames Valley Constabulary area nor with the Spotlight Initiative in Strathclyde.

When the police have done their job, then, as compassionate private citizens, compassionate politicians, compassionate social workers, compassionate clergy, compassionate pressure-groups and compassionate charities, we can do ours.

The 'Causes' of Crime and Quality-of-Life Offences

The personal and environmental influences that interplay in the present and have interplayed in the past, to form the context in which a person decides to act in an unlawful, immoral or offensive way, are in every case both numerous and complex.

Environmental influences do not 'cause' crime or any other type of human conduct. Human beings are not the inanimate objects of their circumstances like iron with its own coefficient of expansion, or like instinct-driven creatures in the animate world. Environmental influences do not 'cause' people to behave in one way or another. They make a certain line of conduct easier or more difficult. The term 'cause' has been borrowed from the physical sciences as a rough shorthand for this fact. So long as the word 'cause' applied to social affairs is recognized as nothing but a sometimes useful, sometimes misleading, analogy (and normally I do not hesitate to use the term so long as that is understood) no great harm is done.

In 1931 the national figure on unemployment was 21 per cent. In 1931 there were 208 robberies nationally.

In 1996 the national figure on unemployment was eight per cent. In 1996 there were 72,000 robberies nationally.

Before the 1960s crime was an *option* that by present day standards was very rarely chosen by poor and unemployed people, and England was a safe, law-abiding and—a word often used then and later—'decent' society. The position in many towns and industries was as objectively 'hopeless' then as it was in 1996. But the Pilgrim Trust, reporting in 1938 on the long-term unemployed, said of the Durham miner that his reaction was 'a sturdy refusal to give up'. Neither he nor his sons dealt with their problems by turning to theft, violence, and vandalism against their neighbours. A few were mastered by the sociable and simple drug of alcohol, but the abstinence movement, then still influential, had made great inroads into drunkenness in the mining communities. There was no 'drug scene' in Stanley during the long and hard years of the Depression, when no one could yet know whether prosperity would ever return.[6]

The poverty and unemployment lobbies have *something* to work on. In many very obvious and objective ways unemployment was a much worse experience in the 1920s and 1930s than in 1996. But no doubt in some ways, especially subjectively, poverty and unemployment, at a much higher standard of living in both cases, could be a worse experience in 1996 than it was between the wars.

But imagine as science fiction that an unemployed man in the 1930s could have been told fully and honestly about all the conditions he would have to endure as an unemployed man in the 1990s, with the attitudes of an unemployed man in the 1990s. Would he come to the 1990s or stay where he was? Would an unemployed man of the 1990s change places with an unemployed man in the 1930s?

The answer that the poverty and unemployment lobbies give —their case logically depends entirely upon it—is that the 1990s' man would chose the 1930s because he would conclude that unemployment in the 1930s was in some ways decisively and massively better than the 1990s.

It is no good those lobbies saying that the comparison cannot be made, and therefore the point is nonsense. Their whole argument depends upon *their* having implicitly made such a comparison and calculation, and coming to that conclusion.

To make their case that the massively higher level of crime is due to some massively worse condition of poverty and unemployment *in some sense or another*, the poverty and unemployment lobbies have to use the utmost ingenuity and diligence, and remain robustly neglectful of the logical principles summed up as 'Occam's Razor', that the simplest explanation is the best.

It is only by ignoring or dismissing figures that do not suit their case, and inflating those that support it, and only by tortuous, factitious interpretations, that influential modern centres of 'research' and 'expert comment' in academia and the serious media can succeed to their own satisfaction in attributing the difference between 1996 and 1931, 346 robberies in 1996 for every one 1931, to an overwhelmingly powerful increase in the detriments of unemployment and poverty as the 'causes' of crime.

Unfortunately, with their 'scientific' authority, they have succeeded in persuading many people of perfect good-will as well.

Poverty or unemployment as a 'cause' of crime, except as a metaphor to be used with the mind always on tenterhooks, cuts all the ground from underneath any sort of religious or even moral view of man.

Applying the word 'cause' literally to human beings, in its physical-sciences' sense, justifies any degree of either indoctrination or social control that might be necessary as counteractive 'causes'.

Alternatively (the currently dominant direction) as no-one can possibly be responsible for what his environment makes him do, all education is dismissed as 'manipulation', all social control as 'repression', and all morality as senseless—the fashionable philosophy known as 'post-modernism'.

Astonishingly, some of the softest targets for the doctrine that 'social, and especially material, conditions cause crime' have been found in the ranks of the 'progressive' clergy up to the highest levels. Does it not strike them that the way in which the unemployed in 1931 *thought about* the right and wrong ways they should *deal* with their unemployment—as individual human beings in their own right, and not as flotsam and jetsam on the sea of 'social conditions'—might explain the difference between 1931 and 1997 somewhat more simply and convincingly? Might not such an explanation sit more easily, into the bargain, with the religious and moral doctrines they otherwise claim to profess?

The Incentives to Commit Crimes

Environmental influences are broadly of two types. On the one hand there are the incentives to behave under the sway of one's impulses or in the pursuit of one's own interests without regard for the consequences to others (and sometimes regardless of the consequences to oneself). These incentives to behave badly can all in one way or another be grouped under the heading of 'frustration'.

If we feel frustrated economically we are tempted to steal or defraud. If we feel frustrated emotionally, we may engage in bizarre behaviour to be at least noticed by the person who is neglecting us. If we are physically massive enough, we may compensate for unrequited love with the satisfactions of brutal conquest. If we feel we are insufficiently respected, we may create for ourselves the satisfactions of power and revenge by the destruction and defacement of objects of the people who have slighted or humiliated us. If the supposed authors of our humiliation are too likely to be able to identify us and retaliate, we may simply transfer our aggression to a completely innocent substitute, such as an old lady in the neighbourhood who can fairly safely be robbed and with almost complete safety be insulted—the familiar reaction of 'kicking the cat'.

When 'relative deprivation' is the 'cause', then resources place no ceiling on bad behaviour. Money buys the things that keep people well-fed and warm, that make a home comfortable and beautiful, that enable their diseases to be eradicated or cured, that make us feel we look or smell nice. Having 'plenty of money' makes the management of one's resources less onerous and time consuming. An increase in material resources makes it easier to buy things that are good for you and to be generous to other people. All these things and many more are desirable and may be universally achievable.

But few societies have ever produced a social-affairs intelligentsia like our own that has taken and presses the view that good behaviour is secured by increasing material resources.

Such a theory is contradicted by all human experience, and was rejected by the founder of every widespread and durable world religion or ethical code. Good behaviour, with money or without money, is secured by quite other means. For, empirically speaking, whole populations of very poor people have behaved very well, and whole populations of very rich people have behaved very badly.

People with little money have coped with their frustrations individually and collectively by emphasizing and practising 'virtues'. People with plenty of money can always find frustrations to feed their resentment and bad behaviour, if that is how they respond to life. 'Forget about amateurs like Fergie', a *Sunday Times* 'Profile' reads. 'When it comes to *behaving badly*, Princess Margaret is in a class of her own.' One of her closest friends explains this in terms of her 'relative deprivation' and 'exclusion'. 'Princess Margaret has had to *make do* with what is *left over*. She was *second best*. In a way she had to be *marginalized*.' The 'Profile' columnist adds that the palace establishment 'stabbed her in the back'.[7]

The report may be true or untrue. The point is that it takes for granted the cogency of the argument that frustration '*causes*' bad behaviour. That Princess Margaret has had plenty to complain about in her life is almost certain. But in that respect she is just like—or perhaps even better off than—millions of her fellow-citizens who have not coped with their frustrations by behaving badly.

But when this view of life, that frustration 'causes' bad behaviour, is fed and feeds down to boys and young men in Harlem or Hartlepool, the consequences have been and are neither chic, nor entertaining, nor trivial.

The 'relative' poverty and 'relative' deprivation argument would equally well 'explain' the spread of criminal behaviour in the British business community as a consequence of their comparing their own wealth with that of Saudi princes.

Relative poverty is an incentive to criminal conduct which it is the business of other forces of education and social honour to counteract.

The Disincentives to Commit Crimes

The disincentives to commit crimes include a personal sense of guilt and the emotional discomfort that guilt arouses. People therefore try to implant in others the readiness to feel uncomfortably guilty if they behave badly, and pleasantly virtuous when they behave well. Another disincentive to behaving badly is public disapproval and the consequent loss of benefits associated with being despised, distrusted and disliked. A third disincentive to bad behaviour is police action—the subject of this book.

Even though in this country it needed an American, Charles Murray, to ring the alarm bells,[8] it has now almost ceased to be disputed that something quite profound has happened, in the calculations of the perpetrators, to the balance of the personal rewards and costs in committing criminal acts and acts of subcriminal disorder. The periodic British Crime Surveys (BCS) show a figure of 11 million crimes in 1981. By 1995 there were 19 million.[9]

It was the innovation of victim surveys of the BCS that destroyed one of the main anti-police tactics of the cultural proponents of permissiveness, namely, the tactic of claiming that crime was not really increasing—that the crime figures were simply a creation of the public's 'moral panic', where it was not an illusion deliberately created by police to justify their claims for expanded powers, money, and establishments.

These BCS figures, by confirming the validity of the *trends* in crime shown by the official police statistics of recorded crime, strengthened the case for believing that the official statistics were also a reasonable guide to trends before the BCS figures began to be collected in the 1980s.

According to the official figures, crime in England and Wales shifted decisively upwards from about 1955. Up to 1955 the crime rate had been below 1,000 crimes per 100,000 population, year after year and decade after decade. Yet by 1965 the crime rate had much more than doubled to 2,600, even though 1955-65 had been a period of very low unemployment. The crime rate had much more than doubled again by 1985, to 7,300. The *rise* in the crime rate in the single year 1990-91 was *twice* the *total* crime rate of 1955.

The question of the how far an increase in frustration can explain this rise is a broad and difficult one. Obviously, if someone *feels* frustrated he *is* frustrated. If someone *sees himself* as deprived, he will *act* as a deprived person. Most people, probably, have plenty of reasons for thinking and feeling that they have not the money, the power, the love, the respect, the beauty, the sex appeal or potency, that they think they deserve or would like to have. People differ, however, in the extent to which they allow their feelings of frustration to grow and dominate them. They differ, too, in how they cope with even overpowering feelings of frustration.

What is more important, different *cultures* handle the incipient feelings of frustration and the proper reaction to them in different ways. Some cultures handle them by reducing the level of personal expectations, hopes and wishes. Some cultures handle them as challenges to be met and overcome by human effort and ingenuity. Other cultures handle them by blaming 'deprivation' on other people's (e.g. a witch's or a sorcerer's) lack of compassion, abuse of power and malevolence.

The Balance of Incentives and Disincentives in British Culture

Since 1955 British culture has changed drastically and rapidly in one respect which was fundamental to the way in which frustration is handled. Until the mid-1950s a British male was brought up with the strong demand made upon him that he would become the life-long husband to only one wife; that she would be his sole ever sexual partner; that together they would live in the same home to bring up their children; and that being a husband and father of this kind was a major, if not the major, project of life.

Maintaining that system meant that a very large number of people took a very great interest, not only in how each boy and young man was behaving himself in the here and now, but even more in what his present conduct meant for what he was growing up to be. There was a lot at stake. The fact that many people (especially the very rich) violated the rules, that some rules (such as that of pre-marital chastity) were extremely difficult to monitor and control, and were often evaded, does not prove that the system had no important effects on conduct.

The social effort that went into maintaining the rules was great precisely because sex is a very unruly and difficult thing for the individual and society to deal with.[10] More importantly, sex can mean conception, and (if they are not simply to be disposed of) babies take a lot of looking after.

Quite suddenly and rapidly, in the period from the mid-1950s into the 1990s, British boys and young men began to be released from the heavy obligations and strenuous expectations involved in this culture of lifelong monogamy.

They could now handle their frustrations to an ever-increasing extent as self-regarding individuals. As compared with their predecessors, how boys dealt with their frustrations became to a far greater, and to an increasing, extent nobody's business but their own. At the same time, the culture shifted in the direction of defining difficulty and shortage as 'deprivation'—the withholding by someone else, or some group, or some 'structure', of something to which one was entirely entitled.

Options of anti-social conduct were opened up which had formerly been closed off to boys and young men. The culture of personal effort in the face of difficulties was being dissipated. It was gradually replaced by a culture of sullen resentment that one's difficulties were other people's fault that they had to remedy ... or else. Regard for, and the reality of, the reactions of people permanently able to make their life more comfortable and pleasant if they behaved properly and less comfortable and pleasant if they behaved badly, their permanent and stable circle of unambiguous kinsfolk, was weakening. Nearly everyone, through their taken-for-granted participation in the culture of lifelong monogamy, had played a part in the maintenance of the system that ensured as far as possible that any baby would have a home and two parents during the long period of its dependency on others during childhood and adolescence. That was no longer the case.

Coincident with the weakening of social control by the kinship system was the weakening of a range of other working-class institutions which had helped close off crime and other anti-social and self-destructive conduct as possible responses to frustration. Friendly societies, the co-operative movement, the Labour Party when it was strongly oriented towards the philosophy of ethical socialism and Christian Socialism, the chapels, the working men's clubs in their educative aspect—all these went into decline.

The chapter on crime and culture in Hartlepool is of general interest in this connection. It is a text-book example, on various important and uncontroversial measures of material and social well-being (the partial exception being unemployment), of the objective sources of frustration being significantly *reduced* during the period of *rising* crime. Hartlepool is even more interesting when we do take the terrible experience of unemployment fully into account. For again, very clearly, it was no worse a problem objectively, and at times much less of a problem during the period of rising crime, than it had been during other extended periods in the history of the town.

But when poverty and unemployment had been dealt with in the context of strong families and other institutions of socialization and social control, then crime, vandalism and teenage hooliganism had remained at low levels.

So long as the family and other institutions were strong, the police, of course, could be both formidable and unobtrusive. (A handful of bobbies at Highbury or Roker Park had nothing very much to do but watch the match; incipient unruliness in the 30,000-strong crowds and more was suppressed by the adult male spectators on the spot. But when they were needed, a few police officers were enough. The most vivid image of this kind of control is the lone 'policeman on the white horse' controlling the vast crowd that invaded the Wembley pitch, I think in 1926.) But from the 1960s, as fewer adult males exercised social control, the rewards became sparser and the risks greater for the remaining males who might attempt to continue to do so. More and more of the burden of social control was thrown onto the police force.

Undermining the Police

The police are obviously only one element in this complex situation. But the police, too, were in an important respect being weakened. In Britain, in Europe and in the United States, there were successful attacks upon what had been the closely inter-related central assumptions of police action—as distinct from social work, medicine, politics, religion or metaphysics.

One central assumption for police action was that when a crime had been committed someone was responsible for it. The law is capable of being upheld only on the *assumption* (true or false) of personal responsibility. The assumption that increasingly displaced it was that a crime was a helpless individual's inevitable reaction to some set of external circumstances.[11] In one of the first books to point out the emergence of the new assumption, and its perverse influence on policing, the criminologist Patricia Morgan provided an extreme but homely example of the contrast between the two assumptions from a simple conversation heard at a bus stop. It concerned a seven-year-old who had been in the process of dismantling the classroom while the teacher stood passively by. 'Can't you stop him?', asked a mother. 'He comes from a broken home.' 'Well', said the mother, 'he can bloody-well learn, can't he?' The mother's assumption was that by treating the child as responsible for his actions, he could be changed. The teacher's was that the situation *from which she gratuitously excluded herself and the school* had simply to be tolerated, and that it was dominated by what was negative, hopeless and irreversible.[12]

In 1954, nearly 20,000 children under the age of 14 were found guilty of offences. In 1994 the crime figure was eleven times higher than in 1954; but the number of children under the age of 14 who were found guilty of offences was six times lower. As Charles Murray writes (whose calculation this is), the *motives* to deal with the young as people not responsible for their actions were noble. The *effects* have crept up on us, as successive generations of young offenders have come to think that they can get away with almost anything.[13]

A police force can act meaningfully on the first assumption—that the sane adult, and gradually the growing infant and child, can be held responsible for what he does. But 'policing' does not make sense on the second assumption—that the individual is the creature of his (non-police) environment. On that assumption, so long as the circumstances remain unchanged, the number of criminals and criminal acts will remain unchanged. Policing, in that case, loses its moral justification. Equally, policing loses its practical justification—the police are helpless to do anything about crime. All they can do is to go through the motions of controlling it—at best without themselves succumbing to corruption and to the abuse of what they legally have uniquely in their hands—'the dangerous drug of violence', as the nineteenth century philosopher Bernard Bosanquet called it.

Neither of these assumptions, of 'the responsible individual' and 'the sovereignty of circumstances', has ever been totally dominant anywhere. But the rapid substitution, in the last forty years, of the notion of 'personal responsibility in all circumstances' by the notion of 'circumstances determining the actions of all persons', effectively undermined the authority of the police in the estimation of the public. As importantly, it sapped the confidence of police personnel themselves in the legitimacy and effectiveness of their policing function.

Another central assumption was that police forces existed only to protect the law-abiding citizen and apprehend the suspect. Undermining the notion of personal responsibility and replacing it with the notion of external causation (from which policing itself was implicitly excluded as irrelevant to conduct, just as the school-teacher had excluded herself from the child's situation) obscured the distinction between victim and culprit, where it did not lead to complete role reversal.

The milder form of role reversal made the old 'victim' into the culprit. For the victim of a crime had created, or had been at the least a willing upholder of, the circumstances that 'forced' the thief, the malingerer, the rioter, the vandal, the lout, the terror- ist, to act in the way he did. The old 'culprit' was thus the new victim—the victim of the circumstances through which society had forced him to adopt his anti-social or self-destructive ways. Very few crimes (notably rape) escaped this tendency towards the understanding of the—in some ways—blameless miscreant at the expense of the—in some ways—guilty victim. A Church of England vicar working on Meadow Well estate, the scene of rioting and arson in September 1991, described as 'crap' the idea that an element in the estate's problems might be a deficiency in moral teaching. The causes lay, in his view, in the material poverty of the residents.[14]

The stronger form of role reversal went further still. In some societies, not all, the laws of the state and the rules of its voluntary associations were widely considered to be, on the whole, 'good'. Where they were not good enough there was a 'good' way to change them by using the rules that governed changes in the laws or rules. Law abidingness—respect for the rules of membership and the customs of social intercourse—was therefore in nearly all circumstances itself considered to be 'good'. In some societies the laws and rules of conduct were thought to be so good that they were worth dying for.

From the 1950s these ideas were progressively weakened. In their place two notions were simultaneously propagated— sometimes, incongruously, by the very same people. The first notion was that there was nothing on a societal level to choose between the way of life of the English, the Irish, the Russians, or the Comanche. At a personal level, there was nothing but 'life-styles', none of which could be graded above or below any other in terms of practical viability or moral worth.[15]

The second, contradictory, notion was that few if any societies have matched in the immorality of their way of life the slave-owning and then the capitalist 'Amerika', or England with its repressive legacy of brutal and selfish imperialism abroad, and élitist, sexist and exploitative 'Victorian values' at home—and the present disgraceful manifestations in both Britain and the United States of homelessness, racial prejudice, gender discrimination, unemployment, poverty and neo-colonialism. In spite of the extreme objective difficulties in making out the case, unceasing propaganda has been remarkably successful in establishing in the public mind the view that rising criminality and rising sub-criminal disorder have been the result of the severer hardships in terms of poverty and unemployment that recent generations in Britain have experienced as compared with their predecessors. No doubt this is partly due to the fact that, as Hitler argued in *Mein Kampf*, ordinary people know how to assess little untruths, but they do not know how to cope with really big ones.

The success achieved in spreading these two sets of ideas can be illustrated by one example from someone with relatively little influence on the intellectual life of Britain, and by another example purporting to be from a position near the peak of intellectual influence in Britain.

The first example deals with the idea that there is nothing to choose between one way of behaving and another, and therefore all attempts to give special protection through the laws or nation-wide customs to one way of life rather than another, and to ensure the enforcement of those laws if necessary through police action, is senseless if not absurd. I was once travelling on the night coach from London to the North, having attended the annual Remembrance Day service at the Merchant Navy War Memorial at Tower Hill. In a neighbouring seat was a 25-year-old woman from a County Durham colliery village with her young family. In the conversation it transpired that she had taken a GCSE in history, specializing in the Second World War. Her confident verdict, from which she could not be budged because she had an academic qualification in the subject, was that there had been nothing to choose between the evils and virtues of the combatants. They both had, equally, right on their side. They were both equally at fault. From what she had been taught at school, she knew that the origins, the course, and the result of the war between Nazi Germany and the allies 'was six of one and half-a-dozen of the other'.

The second example deals with the idea that certain values associated with the British way of life are especially repugnant to any humane person. The success of the attack on 'Victorian values', which denigrates nineteenth century British society, or contemporary British society, or both, is evidenced by the fact that, according to a recent report in *The Sunday Times*, a professor at the University of Oxford asserted that 'the Victorians hanged young people for stealing a handkerchief'.

Queen Victoria reigned from 1837 to 1901. During those sixty-four years no person, young or old, was ever legally hanged for stealing a handkerchief, or for anything remotely resembling that offence. Even if the report had addressed the period when the number of capital offences on the statute book was at its highest—*before* Queen Victoria came to the throne—it would be very difficult for anyone to unearth even a single example of the sort of event attributed to the Victorians as characteristic of 'Victorian values'.

Whether or not it was actually made, the important point is that this ludicrous assertion could be widely disseminated in 1996 by one of the country's most widely read and most highly respected newspapers, backed with all the authority of an Oxford University professor as its source.[16]

As a corollary to the notion that British society was irredeemably corrupt, the criminal was elevated to social hero. The influence and spread of this idea was out of all proportion to the numbers of those propagating it. By flouting its rules the ram-raider was in the active vanguard of those who would save society by the revolutionary transformation of its laws, or by doing away with them altogether. By refusing to conform to society's demands on him to be sober, healthy, industrious and independent, the drug addict was saying 'No!' to the intolerable injustices lying behind those demands, and perpetuated to the extent that he complied with them. For that idea to have dire effects for social order and the effectiveness of consensual policing, it need not be believed or even be widely known in the population generally. It was sufficient that it should filter down to the young criminal or drug user himself. Not surprisingly, he was very receptive to it.

A third assumption formerly underpinning police action was that the state, through the armed forces externally and normally the police internally, has the right to use legally-defined, minimum force as a last resort against the criminal, and the criminal has no right to use force against the police. The German sociologist Max Weber argued that a state only existed if and in so far as it had succeeded in persuading the population to *consent* to *its* use of force (including against themselves if they break the state's laws) and *not* to consent to the use of force by anyone else except with its permission or prescription, the only exceptions being narrowly circumscribed cases of self-defence.[17]

In western liberal democracies this legitimacy—this willing acceptance of the rarest possible resort to the minimum of required coercive social control ('it's a fair cop, guv!')—is based on two claims. The first is that the rules governing the state's own use of force prevent it from interfering in the lives of law-abiding citizens (the proper meaning of 'the rule of law'). The second is that a society works with a minimum of force where only people unambiguously authorized by the state, working within strictly defined and enforced rules emanating from a government regularly replaceable by universal suffrage, have the right to use it. The use of only *official* force, consciously controlled, is seen as being necessary to suppress the far worse consequences of the spiralling use of private force.

But in the past forty years this legitimacy has on the whole been tentatively extended, though with ebbs and flows, to the use of violence by groups with a self-defined social grievance or a moral cause—housing-estate rioters, violent pickets, nationalists, animal-rights campaigners, students who will not allow a person with 'undesirable' views to speak on their campus, poll-tax protesters and so forth.[18] The most important advances in the acceptance of the idea of legitimate private violence was during the miners' strike of 1984-85, but there were many other 'good causes' over the period, especially from the late sixties, that assisted in its spread.

Since the late 1950s the successful weakening of the underpinnings of policing has been the work of experts in the social sciences; of dramatists; of novelists; and of an intellectual élite in general which has been provided with the new megaphone of television, film and recorded popular music.

The Idea of 'Permissiveness'

Outside the police forces, but profoundly affecting their outlook and that of the general public, were changes that took place from the 1950s onwards, both in the expansion in the number of government-employed social workers of one kind or another and, not less importantly, in the ideas that guided social-work practice.

Social work originated in care for the physically and mentally ill or handicapped, the widow, the orphan, the sober, conscientious workman without employment, and the victims of other people's bad behaviour like the abandoned mother. The type of such a social worker was the hospital almoner.

Police forces have been mainly agents of social control, but incidently they have been agents of socialization also. Social workers have been brought closer to the police in that, from the 1950s onwards, they were increasingly appointed to be mainly concerned with the *belated socialization* of people who had not been successfully socialized or who had been mal-socialized as children by society's other institutions and influences—by the family, the school, the chapel, the Rave, the football team, the dance class, children's books, records, television programmes and videos, by *My Darling Clementine* or by *Reservoir Dogs*.

'Socialization' is the process which is intended to produce a person who will be technically equipped with the skills and internal motivations to do what it is socially appropriate and useful for him to do. He will be able and *he will want to do* what he ought to do. 'Social control', on the other hand, is the process through which people are induced to do, and in the case of coercive social control, *made to do* what they ought to do, or are deterred or prevented from doing what they ought not to do. The two processes come together in one important respect. A crucial element of socialization is the inculcation of the attitudes which make the person sensitive and amenable to *low-level* social control, to allowing his 'deviant' conduct to be 'nipped in the bud'. One of the most famous scenes in the history of the cinema is of Gene Kelly 'singing in the rain'. Although in the film he plays the part of a celebrity, he stops, and moves obediently and sheepishly away in response to the mere appearance of an ordinary constable. The constable had done nothing. He had just stood there. He had 'made his presence felt'. That was the United States in 1952.

Clearly, few people have an interest in using their resources in assisting other people to pursue activities which they regard either as indifferent or damaging to the interests of themselves as givers, or as damaging to the recipients. Most people do not want to facilitate, through supporting with their taxes or charitable contributions, the free choices of people whose socially- or self-destructive conduct is the expression of failed socialization. The socializing element of the social-work profession grew on the basis of the claim—and it was the only basis on which the public would conceivably have paid social workers' salaries—that their treatment of the under- or mal-socialized client would be beneficial to the public. It was highly desirable, of course, that it should at the same time benefit the client. But the benefit to the client was secondary. It was not paramount, as it had been in the work of the hospital almoner.

The leading and highly influential theoretician of socialization at the beginning of the expansion of 'socializing' social work in Britain, the rest of western Europe and the United States, was the American sociologist Talcott Parsons. He put the common sense of the ordinary successful parent, teacher or manager into a form that made it sufficiently high-flown, and seemingly difficult enough, to be incorporated into university courses, and seemingly technical enough to be available to bolster the claims to expertise of groups of workers desiring professional status.

In a nutshell his theory was this: Human beings depend upon one another if they are to survive. This is particularly true of the human infant, with its long period of helplessness. But most babies are born into, and most adults live in, societies which provide much more than the means of bare survival. Some societies have evolved systems that provide their members with a more or less secure and more or less vast array of material goods and educational, spiritual, emotional and other experiences. They have also evolved systems that tend to reduce famine, plague, rapine and war. But the systems that produce the benefits, and the systems that reduce the horrors, work only in so far and for as long as people are competent and well-motivated enough to maintain and improve them.

James Madison, the constitutional theoretician,[19] was therefore too optimistic when he said that 'if people lack sufficient virtue for self-government nothing less than the chains of despotism can restrain them from destroying and devouring one another'. For, Parsons argued, if the people lack sufficient 'virtue'—the trained abilities and ingrained motivation to act 'well' and 'efficiently' in relation to their fellows—no despotism, no policing, by itself can come anywhere close to maintaining the systems of a productive and safe society. Socialization is crucial. Social control can only operate on people who are socialized to respond to it. Coercive social control can only be effective if it has to deal with nothing but the margins of the conduct of the majority, and when the under-socialized or mal-socialized form only a very small minority of the population.

But in terms of what is pragmatically successful, *how* are people socialized? In answering that question at the highest level of generalization Parsons dealt with two states of affairs: that of conduct in conformity with society's operating systems and that of conduct not in conformity with—'deviant' from—society's operating systems. How do you get people out of their deviant behaviour into conforming behaviour?

Formalizing the empirical experience of the mother of every baby, Parsons said that the person doing the job of socialization has to start from where the deviant is (a baby being in Parsons' sense a 'deviant' to be socialized into 'conformity'). The socializer has to be *in the first instance* 'permissive'. ('Permissive' probably entered the vocabulary of the social worker and then of the media generally in the 1960s as a result of Parsons' use of the word in the 1950s.) She must 'take the person (including a baby) as she finds him'. It is only by interacting with the 'deviant' on his own terms and at his own level that a beginning can be made in moving him towards conformity. If the baby says 'A-goo!', you say 'A-goo!'. If the baby defecates on the carpet, you clean up the mess and otherwise ignore the incident. The mother starts by applauding the baby when it burps, then allows the child to burp with an apology, then prohibits any burping at all. The same considerations apply to the belated socialization of the drug addict or juvenile delinquent. The relationship is first established on the deviant's terms, *but only as part of the socializer's strategy of socialization*. The deviant identifies with the socializer, but the socializer only appears to identify with the deviant.

The socializer moves on to the next stage, still controlled by the strategy of the socialization process. The socializer now makes demands on the baby, the delinquent or the drug addict to conform. But she maintains the relationship in the face of lapses in the deviant's conduct. Parsons calls this the stage of 'support'.

Using the leverage of the material and emotional benefits the deviant enjoys in the relationship that he would lose if it broke down, the socializer now demands conforming conduct in terms of skills, attitudes and performances. Parsons implies that the socializer is now firmly in control of the relationship as a role model with whom the former deviant identifies, for he describes the next stage as 'the denial of reciprocity'—the former deviant now has to give more than he is given.

The former deviant is then moved on to the next stage. His conforming conduct depends no longer mainly or exclusively upon his relationship with the socializer. Parsons calls this fourth and final stage 'the manipulation of rewards'. Because the former deviant is fully socialized he will respond in the conformist manner, overwhelmingly without the necessity of coercive social control. He will respond appropriately to the non-coercive sanctions, positive and negative, that conformist society applies to foster certain skills, attitudes and technical and moral performances and suppress others. He will accept that it is right that he should be prevented from breaking the rules. That is what being successfully socialized means.[20]

The basic outline of Parsons' theory of the need for and means of securing successful socialization was identical to John Dewey's theory of education, with more emphasis on society's interests than is found in Dewey. The teacher must start from where the individual pupil is. He must co-operate with the pupil. But this is only to facilitate the achievement of the teacher's task of making the pupil more competent and co-operative—more useful to himself and others. The teacher uses his insight to help 'organize the condition of the experience of the immature'.[21] One of the teacher's most important lessons, says Dewey, is that of 'mutual accommodation and adaptation'.[22] Dewey had been writing on education since 1897 and was in the influential chair of philosophy at Columbia University from 1904, but his type of 'progressive' education did not become widely influential until the 1930s. By 1938 he was expressing alarm that his doctrines were being misunderstood and misapplied to justify teaching which abandoned the child to its own what he called 'mis-educative' experiences, and to condone such a child's inevitable backwardness and misbehaviour. Dewey insists that the teacher, not the pupil, is 'the engineer of the situation'.[23]

In the 1960s the centre of gravity of Dewey's doctrines was decisively shifted in the direction he had abhorred and had warned against (he died in 1952), but which in some ways they invited—teacher passivity on the one hand, pupil aimlessness and self-centredness on the other. During the same period Parsons' paradigm of socialization, seemingly immune from misuse to justify anti-social selfishness, was also almost completely subverted.

The Revolt Against Respectability

From late in the 1950s—let us say from the publication of Norman Mailer's 'The White Negro'[24]—there was a distinct change in the receptiveness of the public to the idea that western societies sentenced everyone to 'slow death by conformity, with every creative and rebellious instinct stifled'. To comply with its rules was to allow oneself to be 'trapped within the totalitarian tissues' of society. The only life-giving answer was to 'divorce oneself from society, to exist without roots, to set out on that uncharted journey with the rebellious imperatives of the self'. The psychopath in all our natures ought to be encouraged.

Mailer used the same argument to espouse the cause of the graffiti artist, whose personal exuberance and creativity defied the impersonal oppression of the facades they decorated. Old fashioned sociologists from the 1950s continued to protest that unchecked graffiti were a clear signal to both the law abiding and the lawless that the forces of law and order were losing control. By their daily strengthening message of defiance, they invited worse lawlessness.[25] But such interpretations of what was happening went ever more deeply out of fashion.

What if a pair of 18-year-olds, nurturing their psychopathy, beat the brains out of someone serving behind the counter in a sweet-shop? Mailer does not hesitate in his answer. 'One murders not only a weak fifty-year-old man but an institution as well, one violates private property, one enters into a new relation with the police ... The hoodlum is therefore daring the unknown, and no matter how brutal the act is, it is not altogether cowardly.'[26]

By 1967 R.D. Laing's *The Politics of Experience* could be what Myron Magnet calls 'an instant classic of élite culture'.[27] Normal education and socialization amounted to the murder of the soul, Laing asserted. In a mad society, those who participate are the insane ones. The truly sane end up in mental institutions. A version of Laing's doctrine was popularly disseminated when Ken Kesey's *One Flew Over the Cuckoo's Nest* was made into a film. Jack Nicholson, playing Kesey's hero, has feigned madness in order to be transferred from jail to what he thought would be the easier life of the mental hospital. The patients are simply the victims of past and present oppression and repression. The hero from the prison restores them to healthy humanity by, among other things, smuggling a prostitute into the institution for the male patients. The hospital—society—solves the problems a sane interloper poses by lobotomizing him.

The passive way out of society was advocated and first became widely known with the publicity given to the so-called 'beat generation'.[28] The use of illegal drugs was increasingly represented as liberative and mind-enhancing, not addictive and stupefying. In the 1960s the expanding media of television and magazines, and the recovering but culturally metamorphosed medium of film, were disseminating diluted but pervasive versions of the counter-cultural message. Within a few years, and almost across the board, the anti-law anti-hero, whether passive or active, replaced the model family and the heroic upholder of personal virtue and of community values in the cinema and television drama.

In the first instance these ideas titillated middle-class intellectuals. I recall with what enthusiasm a young vicar recommended *One Flew Over the Cuckoo's Nest* to me as a tract for the times. They spread more gradually, and through various channels, to one generation after another of school children and adolescents into the housing areas where they would do most damage to personal and local life.

The British universities had been greatly expanded in the wake of the Robbins' report of 1963, supplying enlarged audiences receptive to literature that would legitimize their new opportunities for self-centred 'fulfilment'. The new media of communication were avid for taboo-breaking (and therefore entertaining) material, whether the taboos concerned religion, sex, drugs, education, 'art' or politics. Civil rights and the Vietnam war were radicalizing America's white campuses and the African-American. To supplement home-grown counter-cultures, films and television programmes consumed in Britain were being fed by pro-drug, anti-police events and attitudes in the United States.

Police authorities increasingly found themselves, therefore, confronted both in the United States and this country with new academic, church, political-party and social-services establishments. These establishments took a much lower view than had their predecessors of the worth of their own society as compared with the known or possible alternatives.

But to the extent that the 'deviant' cultures of crime and drugs were justifiable, and to the extent that the 'conforming' culture was the incorrigible origin of madness, homelessness, the annihilating wars of napalm and agent orange, political corruption, economic exploitation, police brutality, racial oppression, the subjugation of women, and neo-colonialism, where did the duty of the socializing teacher, clergyman, and social worker lie? At the very least it lay in protecting the mis-labelled deviant in the 'permissive' phase of socialization—in *justifying* the conduct of the deviant to the wider society, not in *altering* it (but with the salary of the social worker, who has turned his function inside out, still being paid by the law-abiding citizen). Every abuse of police authority, every misdemeanour by any individual police officer, every example of police brutality, and of course all cases of proven and alleged police corruption were treated as evidence, not for the undisputed need for specific reforms and remedies, but simply as grist for the anti-police mill.

From the mid-1950s, therefore, the police found themselves *both* losing the 'little platoons' of the community which had been responsible more than they ever could be for keeping basic law and order *and* operating more and more within an élite cultural environment which was unfriendly to them (an élite culture which the underclass criminal, the rioter, and drug addict silently endorsed with delight). This was so, even though among the general public, and according to their values (that were certainly eroding, but less quickly than those of the cultural élites), the police continued to command support to a far higher degree than any of the proponents of the new view of the deviant—whether those proponents were among the new social workers, the progressive clergy, university and polytechnic sociologists, or anti-police journalists or politicians.

Police forces in part chose to adapt, and in part were legally required to adapt, and in any case had no option but to adapt, to the new environment of the blunting of the old instruments of socialization and social control, and the sharpening of the weapons of those attacking the police.

In the face of growing crime, the weakening of other means of social control, and a hostile intellectual culture, the police could scarcely become more consensual or permissive than they had been under the old circumstances. But they could hardly escape, either, becoming increasingly receptive themselves to the voices that were undermining their legitimacy.

In important respects the traditions of the British police officer in particular created a spurious and deceptive congruence between what he had always tried to do and the demands of his attackers. Police officers have always been aware that over-reaction can exacerbate the situation or event they are trying to control. 'Minimum force' has been a leading rule of British police forces ever since Sir Robert Peel established the first of them on modern lines in 1829. The tendency of British colonial policy was always in favour of what is now called sensitivity to the 'community' and more generally and strongly 'multi-culturalism', and this policy fed back into policing at home, just as Peel's vision of 'keeping the peace by peaceful means' fed into colonial policy.[29]

Burglary and theft account for about three-quarters of all recorded crime. Between 1954 and 1994 the clear-up rate for these two offences halved. During the same period the odds on a convicted criminal being sent to prison fell by 80 per cent. 'Quite simply, it became safer for criminals to commit crime.'[30]

So long as all police forces moved in the same direction, it was not only technically, it was in principle, impossible to tell whether permissive policing was more successful than less-permissive policing in controlling crime and disorder. It was quite possible, therefore—and it could not be tested and shown to be either true or untrue—that although crime was rising rapidly during the period of the cultural changes discussed above, crime was being kept at the slowest possible rate of increase in so far as it could be controlled by any actions within the powers of the police.

But in the early 1990s some police forces began to question the effectiveness of the policing that had become commonplace. Those who did so were encouraged by a new generation of social scientists who were taking a hard look at the contemporary scene—which amounted, especially in the United States, to the wreckage of the physical fabric of substantial parts of formerly great cities, the explosion of drug use beyond alcohol and nicotine, and the more-or-less unremitting growth of crime.[31]

Ever more people felt ever more confident that they were correct in their feeling that crime was an increasing problem, and wondered whether the police were, indeed, doing as much as they could to combat it. Studies began to appear of the effects of 'new' (or of reinstituted pre-1960s) policing traditions, especially those that explored the possibility that one way to reduce serious crime was to attack sub-criminal social disorder.[32]

The following contributions are assessments of the new consensus on the current seriousness of the problems of crime, drugs, and quality-of-life offences, not least for the health of the economy, and accounts of the ways in which different police forces have envisaged and acted upon (or remain sceptical about) policing that is, or is once again, low-level, confident, and where possible tolerant, but where called for minimally robust.

The intention of this volume is not to press a case. Like others in the series, it is to start a discussion which brings open minds to bear on the ascertainable data of a neglected matter of emerging and urgent public concern.

Crime is Down in New York City: Blame the Police

William J. Bratton

NEW YORK City, a city that only three years ago had a reputation as 'the crime capital of the world' is now being lauded as one of the safest big cities in the world. How did this quick turnaround happen? Blame it on the police. The men and women who make up the New York City Police Department (NYPD) are principally responsible for the dramatic crime decline that continues today in New York City. Over the past three years, the City's crime rate has dropped by 37 per cent. The homicide rate alone has plummeted over 50 per cent.

To truly appreciate the significance of the dramatic crime decline in New York City, it is important to take a walk back through time to understand how New York City gained its reputation as the 'crime capital of the world' in the first place. It is also important to understand how American policing has changed over the past quarter century to effect the decline in the crime rate presently being experienced in cities across the nation.

The Professional Era

During the 26 years I have been involved in American law enforcement, there have been several very significant changes in policing throughout the United States. I entered policing during the 1970s, a time in America when the Vietnam War was still raging. Huge demonstrations were occurring. We had just come through the race riots and resultant civil rights era of the sixties and were fast becoming a much more permissive society. Coupled with this was the nationwide phenomenon of deinstitutionalization of our mental institutions, many of whose former patients became the 'homeless' populations of our inner cities.

Simultaneously, American society and its cities' streets were becoming more disorderly and fear-inducing. American policing was also moving into a new era called 'The Professional Era,' which ironically reduced police presence and control of the streets simultaneously with the new social disorder problems that would provide so much fear and crime in the 1980s and 1990s.

The Professional Era of policing is best defined as the time police relied on what I call the 3 R's: Rapid Response, Random Patrol and Reactive Investigation. As we began to take advantage of emerging technologies like the 9-1-1 system[1] and computer-aided dispatch, police also began to rely upon motorized patrol, replacing the foot patrol officer in most American cities. The ever expanding number of 9-1-1 calls required us to take police off walking posts and put them into cars so officers could rapidly respond to the growing number of calls the system was creating. When not on call, these cars would randomly patrol, hopefully preventing and deterring crime. And as they had always done, once something did happen, police reacted and investigated.

There was an old television show called Dragnet that best epitomised the Professional Era of Policing. Dragnet's main character, Sergeant Jack Webb, was famous for his style of questioning a witness or taking a citizen complaint. He was best known for one famous line: 'Just the facts Ma'am, just the facts.' This line was typical during the Professional Era which called for no personal touch and required little personality. The almost computer-generated voice which the fictitious Sergeant Webb used ironically fitted this period's environment characterized by an increasing use of computers throughout the policing profession. The policing style of the 1970s was going to be the end-all policing methodology; objective, detached and impersonal. During the Professional Era, by focusing on process and not results, police were going to finally be able to successfully control crime using modern technology, rapid response and better management systems.

What happened, however, was quite different. This new type of modern-day policing was ill-prepared for the large volume of calls that were generated by the 9-1-1 system. Most major American cities were overwhelmed. As other city services were declining, the police became the catchall. Dial 9-1-1 and they would come.

Police had more and more calls and less time to investigate, less clearance and solving of crime. And perhaps most importantly, the police had less time to interact in a positive way with members of the community.

And then came the 1980s, a time characterised in the United States by the growing phenomenon of drugs. Drugs, particularly cocaine and the emerging crack cocaine, came into vogue in the mid-1980s. With the drugs came guns, increasingly more powerful weapons such as semi-automatics with fifteen and seventeen rounds instead of the old thirty-eight with five or six rounds of ammunition. Drug-related gun violence, especially among youth, became a mean reality. In what we once thought were safe areas of our cities arose random violent crime. When New York City experienced this in the late 1980s and early 1990s, it began to scare everybody. The problems and violence of the ghettos suddenly seemed to be everywhere. Nobody seemed safe. As noted by George Kelling, co-author of the broken windows article, we had effectually de-policed the streets of our cities.[2]

The Evolution of Community Policing

The late 1980s saw some police researchers and police leaders beginning to realize that some of the basic assumptions behind the Professional Era were flawed. The effects of rapidly responding to crimes were muted because research showed it took people almost 10 minutes to decide to call the police in the first place. And police riding in air-conditioned squad cars, rapidly going from call to call, did not make people feel safer. In fact, it further separated the police from the public, the consumers of police services.

Fortunately, the researchers and practitioners did not stop their work at finding what was not working, but began to look at how to think differently about crime and disorder and develop strategies that would work. From this evolved the concept of community policing. It began all over the country in little bits and pieces culminating in a process at Harvard University's John F. Kennedy School of Criminal Justice where, through a federal grant over a period of several years, police leaders, academics, community leaders, media and politicians came together to talk about policing and the development of community policing. The primary focus was prevention. Policing had come full circle, returning to the concept of being a part of the community, not apart from it, with an emphasis on preventing crime, not just responding to it.

Community policing is a concept that you hear a great deal about. There is a continuing debate as to whether community policing is a philosophy, style of policing or programme and whether it is tough or soft on crime. However, I have always discussed community policing in simpler terms. Just as the three R's best described the Professional Era, community policing is defined by three P's: Partnership, Problem Solving, Prevention. Remember in the 1970s and 1980s police said: 'If you give us additional personnel, equipment and resources we'll take care of your problems and control crime'. This didn't happen because there was no partnership with the community to jointly identify those problems. By working in partnership with the community, other institutions of government and the criminal justice system, police can have a significant impact on crime and disorder. This is the basic premise behind community policing and, when properly applied, it is tougher on crime than anything else we've ever tried. New York City's experience is proof positive of this.

Chasing after those thousands of 9-1-1 calls meant putting bandages on the symptoms of the problems generating the calls. We were not taking effective action to solve the problem that generated the call in the first place. Repeat calls brought police back to the same street corner time and time again to kick the same group of rowdy kids off the corner or address the same domestic violence problem. During the Professional Policing Era, police managers had focused more on measuring response time and time spent on calls. Efforts were focused more on process versus the results of preventing and reducing crime and disorder. Police needed to work harder and more strategically at solving the problem. Community policing enabled police to refocus resources on the most basic reason for our being. The primary reason that London Metropolitan Police force was created by Sir Robert Peel in 1829 was to *prevent* crime from occurring in the first place.

Interestingly, policing's shift from the Professional Era to community policing did not involve a complete changeover. It was more a melding of ideas and strategies. The three R's still have their place for certain crime situations, but not all and not as an overall crime control methodology. Blending the benefits of rapid response and random patrol as well as top notch investigative work with the development of strong community partnerships to solve problems that lead to crime reduction and prevention describes the foundation of policing in America in the 1990s and in New York City in particular.

Policing in New York City in the 1990s

The cover of *Time* magazine calling New York City the Rotten Apple and the 'Do Something Dave' headline in the *New York Post*, begging then Mayor David Dinkins to take action against rising crime and disorder, characterise the state of frustration in New York City in 1990.

How did New York City get such a negative image? How did it become a city so seemingly out of control? In New York City over the previous twenty years, as a result of police corruption scandals in the 1970s, the City consciously opted to remove its police from dealing with anything with the potential for corruption. Police were precluded from entering licensed premises and from giving citations or summonses on many disorder-related street conditions for fear of corruption. The direct result of these restrictions as well as the impact of the Professional Policing model were that the NYPD seemed to withdraw from controlling behaviour on the streets of New York and conditions worsened. Graffiti and other signs of disorder abounded. In the 1970s and most of the 1980s, there was not a subway car in the City that was not completely covered with what some inappropriately described as an urban art form, graffiti. Subway stations became shantytowns for the homeless and aggressive begging increased, exacerbating a climate of fear, compounded by a significant and notorious decline in the quality of life as a whole.

When I first came to New York City from Boston in 1990 as the new Chief of Police for the City's Transit Police Department, I remember driving from LaGuardia Airport down the highway into Manhattan. Graffiti, burned out cars and trash seemed to be everywhere. It looked like something out of a futuristic movie. Then as you entered Manhattan, you met the unofficial greeter for the City of New York, the Squeegee pest. Welcome to New York City. This guy had a dirty rag or squeegee and would wash your window with some dirty liquid and ask for or demand money. Proceeding down Fifth Avenue, the mile of designer stores and famous buildings, unlicensed street peddlers and beggars were everywhere. Then down into the subway where everyday over 200,000 fare evaders jumped over or under turnstyles while shakedown artists vandalised turnstyles and demanded that paying passengers hand over their tokens to them. Beggars were on every train. Every platform seemed to have a cardboard city where the homeless had taken up residence. This was a city that had stopped caring about itself. There was a sense of a permissive society allowing certain things that would not have been permitted many years ago. The City had lost control. It was the epitome of what Senator Daniel Moynihan had described as a process of 'defining social deviancy down'— explaining away bad behaviour instead of correcting it.

The Beginning: Hiring Additional Police Officers

In 1990, Mayor David Dinkins and the City Council realised something had to be done and, with public support, enacted legislation to hire an additional 7,000 police. This hiring was designed to support the community policing programme that was being implemented in the New York City Police Department (NYPD). However, then Police Commissioner Lee Brown wanted to dedicate these 7,000 new young police officers to 1,500 beats throughout the City. The average kid joining the NYPD at that time was a 22-year-old, with only a high school (12 years) education.

- Many of the new hires had never held a job until they applied to the NYPD.
- Many had never even driven a car.
- Many lived outside the City and had never interacted with a minority person.
- Many were under 21 and not even old enough to legally drink.

And these were the 7,000 young police officers who were supposed to solve the problems of New York City, one of the most complex cities in the world, after only six months of police academy training. They were simply not equipped to deal with the city's problems of race, crime and disorder.

Although legislating the hiring of 7,000 additional police officers in the early 1990s was a start and crime began to go down slowly, more was needed. When I became Police Commissioner in January 1994, aware of this deficiency in the previous administration's approach, I undertook a strategic re-engineering of the NYPD that significantly contributed to the dramatic crime reduction and quality-of-life improvement that continues in New York City today.

Re-engineering the Organisation

Like many private corporations that have chosen to re-engineer, the NYPD was an organisation that wasn't living up to its potential. The process of re-engineering requires the setting of clear-cut goals, the restructuring of the organisation to meet those goals and priorities and maximum involvement of Department personnel and outside expertise. Instead of being satisfied with incremental declines in crime, we set ourselves the mission of dramatically reducing crime, disorder and fear. We re-engineered the NYPD into an organisation capable of supporting these goals. We created 12 re-engineering teams covering areas crucial to achieving short- and long-term crime reduction goals such as training, equipment and technology re-engineering teams. We tapped expertise from inside and outside the Department to work on goals and implementation strategies to meet these goals.

Decentralization

In 1994, precinct commanders had very little authority to do anything unless headquarters demanded it. We cut through the 'wedding cake' of centralised hierarchical bureaucracy and put the focus of crime prevention and disorder reduction back on the police in the precincts. In other words, we decentralised policing in New York City.

We pushed responsibility and accountability down, but not to the new, inexperienced beat cop, as the previous administration had done, but rather to the precinct commander level, so that we really had 76 miniature police departments. In view of the complexity of many of New York City's problems the earlier policy had been setting those newly-hired young men and women up for failure by putting them in charge of problem-solving efforts. We changed the focus from that young officer to a more mature (by fifteen years on average) college-educated, veteran police commander who knew how to police the city.

We demanded that precinct commanders place dual emphasis on quality-of-life or signs of crime as well as on serious crime. New York City government had not paid attention to the quality-of-life drinking and minor street crime that citizens experienced every day for over 25 years. As a result the police had stopped enforcing many of the City ordinances which were intended to prevent these violations. I set the macro-level goal of crime reduction and enhancing quality of life, but then let precinct commanding officers manage at the precinct or micro-level by determining how best to do this. In addition to decreasing felony crime, this led to a successful city-wide effort to reduce and prevent graffiti as well as an ongoing elimination of those infamous squeegee pests.

Essential to police enforcing quality-of-life laws for the first time in 25 years was public and political support. New York fortunately had this. In 1994 the newly elected Mayor Rudolph Giuliani had campaigned on the issue of crime and disorder. Upon his election, unlike his predecessors, he authorized the police and their new Police Commissioner to develop and implement strategies to deal with identified problems. As Mayor, he then co-ordinated the activities of other city agencies to support these crime control strategies.

Strategic Crime Fighting

Over a two-year period, the police developed eight crime control strategies to address drugs, guns, youth crime, auto theft, corruption, traffic, domestic violence and quality-of-life crime throughout the City. We developed a geographically-based strategic drug reduction initiative that has been implemented in two areas of New York City with successful preliminary results. We created an innovative system to measure the success of the crime control goals called the Compstat Process. Compstat stands for Comprehensive Computer Statistics. It incorporates four basic premises: timely accurate intelligence data; rapid response of resources; effective tactics and relentless follow-up. In the NYPD, at twice weekly Compstat meetings, the Department's top executives meet. Each command presents the results of their efforts in the previous month compared to their plan for the same period of time.

Changes at the Precinct Level

Before I became Police Commissioner, the emphasis on community policing had resulted in police being assigned to beats in the neighbourhood with the responsibility to solve all crime problems. New police officers, many no more than 20 or 21 years old, were expected to use problem-solving methodologies associated with community policing to address any crime problem, from youths loitering on street corners to rampant drug dealing on their beats. This approach was not working. Some neighbourhoods were so crime-ridden that these young officers could not cope with such complex problems and issues.

Precinct commanding officers had little control over these officers who were assigned via a strictly enforced community policing deployment formula from Police Headquarters. Moreover, resources were more difficult to allocate appropriately under a rigid plan that placed authority and accountability at multifunctional and poorly co-ordinated higher levels. To correct this situation, as previously mentioned, I decided to focus accountability and authority at the precinct commander level. This meant that precinct commanders could decide how many and how best to use beat officers. They were charged with developing problem-solving initiatives because precinct commanding officers had the experience and knowledge to solve complex crime issues. Working within the framework of the Department's eight strategies and Compstat process, they developed problem-solving tactics and deployed officers according to a strategy they developed specifically to work on problems in their precinct.

Commanding Officer Authority and Accountability

Beat officers were just one example of commanding officers' lack of authority over the men and women who worked in their precinct. Specialised units, such as detectives, narcotic units and anti-crime units, were also controlled by other police managers at headquarters. Precinct commanders did not have authority or influence over the assignment and management of these officers. Their hands were tied under a one-dimensional, function-orientated hierarchical police structure. Precinct commanders had been denied greater authority and accountability because it was feared that there was a risk of corruption if headquarter's oversight could no longer be achieved through specialised service provided to the precincts, particularly in traditionally corruption-prone areas.

I ensured that commanding officers were put in charge of their personnel and their assignments. They were given the authority to put together a co-ordinated and focused plan to attack crime in their precinct. They were able to identify crime 'hot spots' and assign necessary patrol officers, detectives, undercover and narcotics officers to these problems. I gave precinct commanding officers the authority and made them accountable. Precinct commanders could bring sufficient deterrents to bear on difficult crime areas, resources could be re-allocated from one 'hot spot' to another within the precinct, results could be measured with greater consistency and reliability, and the precinct was a large enough unit to support its own specialised forces.

The Compstat Meeting

As precinct commanders became the focal point for carrying out their own and the Department's crime-reduction strategies, the Compstat meetings and associated activities became the engine for the effort. They were a product of the favourite four-step philosophy for action of Jack Maple, Deputy Commissioner for Crime Control Strategies and Operations. This philosophy has become a mantra in the Department: (1) accurate timely information, (2) rapid, focused deployment, (3) effective tactics, (4) relentless follow-up and assessment. Twice-weekly Compstat meetings require precinct commanders to be ready to review their up-to-date computer-generated crime statistics and relate what they are going to be doing to achieve crime reduction. These meetings are held at Headquarters in the Department 'War Room' which contains large computer-fed screens and other devices for displaying statistics. One reporter sitting in a Compstat meeting described it as follows:

> Maple called the precinct commanders to the front of the room in turn, questioning, prodding, cajoling and occasionally teasing information out of them. They discussed on-going investigations, special operations and any unusual criminal activity. When the men and women from the 81st Precinct got their call, the precinct commanding officer and his staff were asked to explain a recent spate of shootings.

What's going on, Maple wanted to know. Why are these shootings happening? Is it a turf war? No? Well, somebody's not happy. Maybe they're cranky 'cause its hot outside, but something's happening. When the shooting locations were put up on the huge map projected on the wall, along with those of drug complaints in the precinct, there was a clear overlap. Maple asked what was being done about the drug spots, and one of the narcotics officers said it was a tough area because the business was done inside and there were lots of lookouts. That's fine, Maple said. That's why we're detectives. Tell me what tactics we can employ to penetrate these locations. The detectives said they would try some buy-and-bust operations and maybe get a couple of guys behind the Plexiglas to rat when an arrest was hanging over their heads. Maple wasn't satisfied. I want you back here next week with a plan, he said to the Precinct Captain. Normally each precinct comes in once every four to five weeks.[3]

In order to respond to the kinds of questions posed at Compstat meetings, precinct commanders began bringing with them representatives from other bureaux, such as detectives who were assigned to their precincts. Compstat meetings thus encouraged inter-bureau functional co-ordination.

Making Drug Arrests

We also changed the Department's position against police officers making drug arrests. In the past, it was deemed too risky for street officers to make drug arrests. Since there was a great deal of cash involved in drug transactions, it was thought that the risk of corruption was too great. Heavily supervised special squads had primary responsibility for enforcing drug laws. We changed this policy and even encouraged officers to seek out drug arrests during peak drug dealing times.

Internal Affairs Investigations

Similarly, I changed the way Internal Affairs were conducted in the NYPD. Prior to my tenure, the Head of the Internal Affairs Bureau and the Police Commissioner were sometimes the only two people who had overall knowledge about corruption investigations in the Department. I changed this policy as well, noting that you have to have confidence and be able to trust the integrity of the command staff and precinct commanders. NYPD's 76 precinct commanders in essence ran 76 mini-police departments. Not trusting them with on-going investigations occurring or involving members of their precincts weakened their authority as well as sending a negative message about their trustworthiness. Inclusion became a very strong team builder and motivation tool.

Computer Access for Detectives

Before my tenure, detectives were not allowed to use a number of computer systems because it was thought they would jeopardise the integrity of other investigations. In other words, they were not trusted. These systems included such basic investigatory tools as the computer-assisted robbery system, narcotics databases and on-line warrant system. I gave the detectives access to these computer systems. Integrity was not jeopardised and the NYPD continues to experience some of the steepest crime declines in the country. During my tenure, violent crime has been reduced by 38 per cent and the murder rate has declined by 51 per cent.

Conclusion

However, even as the crime numbers continue to decline today at unprecedented rates across the entire city, there are the sceptics. Some are criminal justice researchers, others are political pundits. They cite theory after theory as to why crime is falling except the one that is of the most significance in New York City: better, smarter and more assertive policing in partnership with the criminal justice system and the community we serve—community policing.

To these critics I unequivocally can say the crime rate did not fall because of the weather. It did not drop due to changing socio-demographic trends. Crime is not down as a result of changes in the economy. The declines may have been affected somewhat by higher prisoner incarceration rates, but the drop in crime in the City has been so precipitous over such a short period of time that the traditional causes of crime, or what we believed to have been the principle causes of crime increases or reductions, just don't apply.

In January 1994, all the young kids in the city did not suddenly become old. All criminals did not suddenly march into jail. 1995 was one of the mildest winters in New York City history: 1994 was one of the worst. Crime went down dramatically in both years, so the weather did not have a significant impact on crime. Murder is not a crime that can be covered up or over-reported. The murder rate has declined by over 50 per cent in New York City because we found a better way of policing. We are results-focused. We are decentralised. We are co-ordinated. We have enough cops and we are using them more effectively. We have partners. We have shown in New York City that police can change behaviour, can control behaviour and, most importantly, can prevent crime by their actions—independently of other factors. We have, in summary, to again quote George Kelling, 're-policed our city streets'.

In response to the criticism that this new policing is too assertive and that citizens are being abused in significantly greater numbers, I am comfortable in saying there is no sustainable evidence to support these assertions. In response, I point to the 166,737 fewer victims of violent crime in the three-year period 1994-96 under our new policing strategies, with our emphasis on prevention rather than reaction, and in public order maintenance as a way of changing behaviour to reduce crime. Did complaints against police increase? Yes they did, but it should be noted that there are over 38,000 police officers making over 300,000 arrests and issuing millions of summonses each year. Compare that activity to the approximately 9,000 citizen complaints that were filed in 1996.

New Yorkers are reporting that they are feeling safer. Residential and commercial real estate markets are booming. The economy has stabilised. Tourism is skyrocketing. New York City is slowly revitalising itself. There are still serious crime problems in New York City that will require additional strategizing and resources. However, as illustrated by the initial success of the newly-implemented geographically-based rather than functionally-based drug reduction strategies in the Brooklyn North and the upper Manhattan areas of the City, the police can have an impact on even long-standing crime problems. The NYPD, or for that matter any successful policing organisation, cannot solve all problems or all crime. However, they should be recognised for what they can do and how well they are doing it today. Fair is fair. We shouldered most of the blame when crime went up. Give us some of the credit when it goes down—and stays down as I confidently predict it will in New York City. And the good news is, 'if you can make it in New York you can make it anywhere'.

Zero Tolerance:
Short-term Fix, Long-term Liability?

Charles Pollard

IN ONE American city, cuts in crime have been achieved which would have been thought miraculous only a few years ago. Murders have fallen by 41 per cent since 1993, robberies by 36 per cent. And it's not just violent crime that has been affected: burglaries and vehicle-related crime have both fallen by over 40 per cent. This and other good news on crime have been attributed to a progressive style of policing adopted by the Police Chief and actively supported by a wide variety of sections of the community. His programme of restructuring has created a police department more responsive to the demands of the public. The city? San Diego, California, of course.

When he took over as Chief of Police, Jerry Sanders set out to provide a responsive, locally-based service, with local police commanders responsible for co-ordinating and managing the priorities of their communities. Partnerships between citizens and police led to greater police accountability, and better assistance for the police from the citizenry. The emphasis was placed on resolving problems long-term, by working with other agencies and organisations. Drug and gang problems were tackled by such means as galvanising ordinary people to join in residents' associations, partnership with the Housing Commission to evict problem residents, and redesigning public areas to reduce crime.

'Shortly after his appointment, Jerry Sanders developed an ambitious agenda to restructure the entire Department to better conform police practices to community standards and principles', says Susan Golding, Mayor of San Diego. 'If current trends hold, the Neighbourhood Policing program [Sanders' initiative] will have reduced crime more than 50 per cent between 1989 and 1996.'

Why have I started this essay by reference to San Diego, when it is supposed to be about policing in New York? It is to correct a common misconception about New York which seems to prevail on this side of the Atlantic, that somehow we too could bring down crime if only we copied the New York style closely enough. Let's be clear: crime is falling in New York and that is good news. But crime is falling elsewhere in America too.

I have particularly chosen San Diego because the fall in crime there is directly comparable in scale to that of New York; and because this has been achieved through a style of policing that is in sharp contrast to that in the 'Big Apple'. The San Diego approach is to work *with communities*; to implement a comprehensive, *holistic approach* that pairs law enforcement with more prevention and intervention programmes from the business/ education and private sectors; and to plan for the *medium and long terms* rather than achieve merely a short-term, quick fix. This approach goes to the heart of what policing is—or should be—all about.

The contrast between this and New York's 'Zero Tolerance' is substantial. Whatever has *actually happened* in the policing of New York—and the theory behind this is described lucidly in William Bratton's paper 'Crime is Down in New York City: Blame the Police'—the *rhetoric about what has happened* has concentrated on the simplistic notion of 'Zero Tolerance'. Whatever the nature of the reforms, the *emotion* underlying them seems to be concentrated on aggression: on ruthlessness in dealing with low-level criminality and disorderliness; of 'rapid response', 'searches, sweeps and arrests' and 'doing a vertical' (raiding an apartment block and arresting all those who cannot account for being there); of confrontational accountability systems within NYPD based on the Compstat meeting, known as the 'war room'; and on the single-minded pursuit of short-term results. There is limited emphasis on the need to work closely with and in communities; nor does the partnership strategy seem aimed so much at the local government agencies (such as education, social services, health and planning) as at the other law enforcement partners such as Prosecutors, the Courts and Prisons. There is seemingly no focus on medium- or long-term needs.

It is important to highlight these distinctions of style because the public debate on policing is in danger of being hi-jacked by the superficial, high profile promotion of 'Zero Tolerance'. This is the term ascribed by politicians and the media to the policing of New York, without proper analysis of what it means and what it has—or has not—achieved. Although William Bratton himself does not use this description in his essay, hardly a day goes by without reference to New York's 'Zero Tolerance' in the news-papers, on the radio or on television. Commentators latch on to it as the latest fashionable label to prescribe the solution to all policing problems.

In fact 'Zero Tolerance'—or rather, the concept of 'Broken Windows' from which it is derived—*is* a hugely important concept in policing; but *it is no more than one fundamental principle of several* that need to be carefully and sensitively woven together if policing is to work well. To get to the roots of this issue, and to understand the New York experience and its wider implications for policing, I will in this paper first explore and contrast the theories of 'Broken Windows' and 'Zero Tolerance'. Secondly, I will examine and analyse the New York experience as presented by William Bratton in his own essay 'Crime is Down in New York City: Blame the Police'. Finally, I will identify the distinctions between policing in New York, and policing in the United Kingdom; and I will explore the lessons we in this country can learn from New York from the debate on 'Zero Tolerance'—and what New York can learn from us.

'Zero Tolerance' and 'Broken Windows' —The Theory

Whilst 'Zero Tolerance' is presented by the media as a new idea invented in New York, it actually stems from the American academic theory of 'Broken Windows',[1] developed by George Kelling and James Q. Wilson back in 1982. I well remember its impact on my own thinking—which still applies today—when I studied it for the first time at the Police Staff College, Bramshill, 15 years ago.

The essence of 'Broken Windows' is that minor incivilities (such as drunkenness, begging, vandalism, disorderly behaviour, graffiti, litter etc.), if unchecked and uncontrolled, produce an atmosphere in a community or on a street in which more serious crime will flourish. This is epitomised by the idea that if a neighbourhood appears to be untended and uncared for—if 'broken windows' and other property are left broken and unrepaired, and disorderly behaviour is allowed to go unchecked—then a cycle of crime will develop and feed off itself.

What will happen is that the neighbourhood will act as a magnet for more serious crime. Drugs dealers and prostitutes will move in. Youngsters on the streets, sensing the lack of order and control, will start committing crime themselves, or turn to more serious crime such as street robbery. Property prices will fall. Respectable, law-abiding people will move out. Possibly they will be replaced by less responsible citizens, some of whom see the area as a haven for crime. So the cycle will continue. As the neighbourhood goes downhill, so crime, disorder and fear spiral upwards.

The 'Broken Windows' principle is fundamentally sound. Where however it becomes more complex and difficult is in the solutions it proposes, and it is here that we need to identify the distinctions from 'Zero Tolerance'.

The expression 'Broken Windows'—and the theory behind it—is essentially about identifying and describing a complex problem; but with some broad ideas about how to solve that problem which I will outline shortly. 'Zero Tolerance', on the other hand, is concerned purely with solutions. The expression imparts both the idea of tackling low-level crime and disorder; and of doing so in a particular way, namely through aggressive, uncompromising law enforcement.

This is the nub of the issue. The 'Broken Windows' theory envisages a solution which includes the enforcement of the law, through arrest and prosecution *where necessary*; but *it will only be effective if applied in conjunction with a wide variety of other police tactics*. Further it is only likely to impact successfully and enduringly on the problem *if pursued in partnership with—and complementary to—the work of other social agencies*. There are two issues here and I will deal with them each separately.

The Police Role in Tackling Disorderly and Untended Neighbourhoods

Dealing with the minor incivilities associated with 'Broken Windows' is much more complex than it seems on the surface. In the first place the law in these areas is often unclear. Conduct which is anti-social, such as vagrants lying on the edge of a pavement when there is still plenty of room for pedestrians to pass, or rowdy youngsters congregating on private property open to and abutting the road, may not be technically unlawful, even if it causes offence to others. People who have been drinking but are not drunk—or, sadly, those who are mentally disturbed and acting in strange ways—may cause anxiety to others but are not necessarily acting illegally. Applying the law to the different types of incivility is not therefore a straight-forward exercise; nor, in a democracy in which people's rights are deemed to be important, should it be so.

And if police do 'go in heavy', what are the implications? Every arrest in the UK takes the arresting officer off the streets for up to four hours: is that a sensible use of police time? And what can the courts do with this type of offender: fine them, when they have little or no money? Or sentence them to imprisonment, when the prisons are already full, and at huge cost to the taxpayer? And what impact does heavy-handed policing—going right up to the limits, or beyond the limits, of legitimacy—have on the community; or on the values and standards of the police officers required to carry it out? Is it likely to increase trust between police and public, or rather to destroy the very relationships that are needed for effective policing?

In fact, the policing of 'incivilities' requires several things. First, it requires police officers on foot patrol: mobile officers in cars are insulated from the street atmosphere and unable to see the problems clearly, let alone deal with them. Second, it requires that officers on foot patrol should be local, identifiable community officers who regularly patrol 'their patch'. Only then can they get to know the people, the problems and the offenders causing the incivilities. Third, it requires that those officers are in sufficient numbers—and part of the same identifiable police team—to have a visible, consistent impact on the problem.

Fourth, it requires the officers to exercise their discretion firmly and effectively. Persuasion will often achieve the desired outcome. Wilson and Kelling in 'Broken Windows' described how good community officers create their own informal policing regime for dealing with incivilities, and I can do no better than quote from their essay:

> The people on the street were made up of 'regulars' and 'strangers'. Regulars included both decent folk and some drunks and derelicts

who were always there but who knew their place. Strangers were, well, strangers, and viewed suspiciously, sometimes apprehensively. The officer—call him Kelly—knew who the regulars were, and they knew him. As he saw his job, he was to keep an eye on strangers, and make certain that the disreputable regulars observed some informal but widely understood rules.

Drunks and addicts could sit on the steps, but could not lie down. People could drink on side streets, but not at the main intersection. Bottles had to be in paper bags. Talking to, bothering, or begging from people waiting at the bus stop was strictly forbidden ... If a stranger loitered, Kelly would ask him if he had any means of support and what his business was; if he gave unsatisfactory answers, he was sent on his way. Persons who broke the informal rules, especially those who bothered people waiting at bus stops, were arrested for vagrancy. Noisy teenagers were told to keep quiet.[2]

The essence of police tactics such as these is the regular, visible presence of the same police officers on foot patrol, using their powers of arrest and prosecution in conjunction with their discretion under the law, acting firmly but fairly and utilising their 'people skills'. They will of course make arrests and prosecute people; but that will be only for overt or persistent breaches of the law and usually as a last resort when other methods have failed. They will liaise effectively with other agencies; and work closely with other specialist police departments charged with investigating and preventing more serious crime such as drug dealing, burglary and robbery, by providing the critical intelligence and information they need.

Policing and Partnership

The second issue is about partnership. No matter how effective the police are in tackling these problems on their own, the results are unlikely to be successful or lasting unless they work in close partnership with the other public service agencies.

This is because the visible signs of decay and disorderliness in a neighbourhood often have many interlinked causes, all of which need to be tackled in a co-ordinated way. Police efforts on their own will have little impact if they deal effectively with the drunks, the vagrants and the anti-social groups of youths, but the neighbourhood is still scarred with broken windows, boarded up buildings, derelict cars, graffiti and litter.

This requires close working relationships between the police and a large number of other agencies: the local refuse collection service; the highways authority; the education and youth departments; the gas and electricity utilities; the social services and probation departments; the planning department; and many others.

But the purpose is not just to ensure that the physical environment is attended to properly. Many of the problems of the neighbourhood will be exacerbated by other issues: the lack of suitable amenities, particularly for young people; poor lighting at night, particularly in areas where people feel unsafe; the presence of individuals or families with special problems; or of neighbours who are constantly 'at war' with each other; the failure to apply crime prevention principles in the design of buildings or of open space; or the failure of some local public services, through fear or disorganisation, to provide the community support that is needed.

There are a whole range of issues that can only be tackled if agencies pool their information, and join together in seeking common, consistent solutions. This is the classic problem-oriented approach to policing as expressed by the highly influential American academic Herman Goldstein in his book *Problem Oriented Policing.*[3]

There are therefore important contrasts of emphasis and style between 'Zero Tolerance' and problem-oriented policing. The former implies emphasis on strong law enforcement and use of the formal criminal justice system; the latter sees the police using a much wider variety of tactics to achieve their objectives, working closely in harmony with the local community and agencies, seeking the underlying causes of problems and trying to solve them for the longer term, rather than merely dealing superficially with the symptoms. This, in fact, is the philosophy which we pursue in my own force, the Thames Valley Police: we call it, simply, 'problem-*solving* policing'.

It is now appropriate to look more closely at the New York experience, to analyse which of these strategies have been applied, and those factors which have influenced the reductions in crime and the improvements in public safety and reassurance.

The New York Experience

Any commentary on policing in New York must start with its uniqueness. 'The Big Apple' is an exceptionally large city, and a very complex one, by almost any measure one could wish to use. Its police force, the NYPD, is a vast organisation which by virtue of its very size and nature is bound to tend towards bureaucracy, long lines of accountability, a hierarchical structure and a culture resistant to change. This is a big challenge for any newly-appointed Commissioner.

When William Bratton took over in 1994, crime and disorder were such that it appeared a city out of control. The crime peak of the 1980s, which he inherited, was higher than anywhere else in America. He vividly recounts in his own essay the pervasive atmosphere of decay, disorder and criminality which greeted him when he arrived to head the City's Transit Police in 1990, a situation which still prevailed four years later on his appointment to the Commissioner post.

The NYPD itself, too, was in a state of inefficiency and confusion. Whilst it had recently been funded to recruit an additional seven thousand police officers, it was still riddled with many lazy, ineffective and—in some cases—corrupt staff, who for far too long had been unaccountable and demotivated. The Mollen Commission had reported on the insular culture and misplaced loyalties prevalent among its police officers. The Department was also in a confused state following the valiant but unsuccessful efforts of Bratton's predecessors to inject community policing into everyday working practices.

Bratton was faced with a crisis. What was needed was inspirational leadership, a huge shake-up of attitudes and accountabilities and a much clearer sense of direction. Bratton provided all three in large measure.

Organisationally, he introduced reforms to bring the NYPD into the 1990s. All of his reforms concerning organisational structures and lines of responsibility—devolvement of responsibility to precinct commanders, the re-alignment of resources under those commanders, and their accessibility to information about internal investigations within their precincts—were measures which police forces in the UK, and many in the US, had introduced many years before. They were long overdue and he did them quickly.

In terms of motivation, Bratton moved to instil trust and empowerment in his officers which were lacking. Under previous régimes, drug arrests on the street had been discouraged because of the fear of police corruption should police officers be allowed close contact with drug dealers. Similar fears lay behind the denial to detectives of access to major computer systems containing information and intelligence which would assist them. These policies epitomised the non-interventionist attitude towards drug dealing, vandalism and low-level disorder which pervaded the NYPD. Bratton moved fast to change these around.

To improve accountability, Bratton introduced the Compstat meeting. This is the grand theatre where precinct commanders are called to account for their recent work, and encouraged (some would say browbeaten) to further efforts. The Compstat meetings also reflect the emphasis on statistical analysis which Bratton brought to NYPD. There are clear benefits to this results-oriented style, not least of which is that it concentrates the mind on the mantra of Jack Maple (Bratton's charismatic Deputy): information, deployment, tactics and follow-up. They are an effective means of directing and concentrating police effort.

The final link in Bratton's reforms was to give NYPD more confidence in itself, and a much clearer sense of purpose. He defined the task of NYPD as 'to reduce crime, disorder and fear' and ensured everyone knew it. There is no more succinct way of setting a police mission, and indeed these are the words which we now use in Thames Valley Police as part of our own organisational 'Aim'.[4]

The significance of this description of the police role should not be overlooked. Many people—including many police officers—see the function of the police as being almost exclusively focused on detecting crime and criminals. This was epitomised by the bland—and wrong—statement in the recent White Paper on Police Reform that 'the main job of the police is to catch criminals'.[5]

The key elements of the NYPD and Thames Valley Police 'mission' statements are that, firstly, both use the term 'reducing crime'. This of course includes within it the detection of crime, but it also includes crime prevention and broader methods of reducing crime. Secondly, both include the critical need 'to reduce disorder and fear'. These two things are, of course, the key problems associated with the 'Broken Windows' theory. They reflect the debilitating fear of crime and disorder—as opposed to its actuality—that many people feel, albeit such fear is often disproportionate to the actual risk of becoming a crime victim. The NYPD mission statement is therefore all embracing and goes to the very heart of policing.

There can be no doubt that, through his reforms, Bratton brought energy, commitment, accountability, higher morale and a sense of direction back into NYPD. An inspirational leader, he gave the organisation a huge shake-up. New York was in crisis; there was heavy political pressure for change; and short-term results—preferably big ones—were needed. His 'no nonsense' approach and superb charismatic skills with the media provided the strongest possible lead to his police officers, and indeed to the people of New York. Bratton provided just what New York needed at the time and should be congratulated on doing so.

There are however two questions which still remain to be answered about this undoubted success. How far do the figures reflect true improvements in the crime rate and in community safety? And what are the future implications for the NYPD of the reform programme?

What Do the Figures Mean?

Whilst no-one can doubt that things have improved significantly and quickly in New York—recorded levels of crime have fallen and people do feel safer—I have to express doubts about the full significance of the statistics. There are many societal factors, as well as policing, which affect crime levels, and it is difficult to be sure which changes have brought which result. For example, it is suggested by some commentators that changes in the crack-cocaine market have influenced the position in New York. I leave that debate to those most qualified to comment.

There is however another issue, and that is about the accuracy of the crime figures. Counting crimes is a notoriously unscientific process. There are always different ways of interpreting crime definitions even with the best of intentions. But, additionally, in NYPD there has been a huge pressure for statistically-based results driven by an uncompromising, ruthless management style, epitomised by the Compstat meeting. Whilst it is essential to have effective processes with which to hold operational police commanders to account, there are huge risks and dangers if it is overdone.

This reminds me of my own early service in London in the 1960s, when a similar culture pervaded the Metropolitan

Police—putting too much emphasis on quantity rather than quality, on internal accountability rather than wider accountability to the public. My first effort as a probationer constable at recording a crime was a valuable lesson in results-oriented gathering of police statistics. Tremulously entering the hallowed domain of the CID office, I was fixed with a glare by the Detective Inspector. 'What do you want?' he demanded. 'I am just putting a theft in the Crime Book, Sir'. 'Is it detected?' continued the DI. 'No, Sir' I replied. 'Well, son, we only put detected crimes in my crime book. I don't need your report, thank you'. That was it.

Since that time, I am glad to say, ethical standards have risen to a very high standard within the Metropolitan Police. However, where there is such clear pressure to produce a specific result, for example an increase in detections or a fall in recorded crime, there will be a commensurate temptation to manipulate figures in order to achieve the 'right' result. 'The numbers game', as it is called by many New York officers, may produce the figures which suggest a desirable outcome. But the emphasis on the figures, as opposed to the outcomes, is the problem.

This is particularly dangerous in any force that has had a problem with corruption: the confrontational atmosphere of Compstat, with its 'war room' and its short cycles of review, is not likely to encourage accurate and ethical reporting. This is particularly so when there seems to be no set of compensating organisational values, incorporating the vital qualities of honesty and integrity, articulated and constantly emphasised from the top and driven down through the organisation's management structure. If it is commonly thought that some senior officers overlook minor transgressions in recording crime, why should junior officers not find it acceptable to bend the rules when giving evidence in court?

Management accountability is something we have been grappling with in my own force, where we too have recently introduced new processes. In addition to detailed performance information published each month, Police Area Commanders receive a day-long visit every four months from the Assistant Chief Constable (Territorial Policing) who goes through the Area's performance in great detail. This is not just about crime levels and detection rates, although that is of course important. It covers the whole range of policing, particularly crime reduction and partnership initiatives, together with concerns such as complaints against police, sickness levels and the management of budgets.

How the Police Area has performed is linked to the Area Commander's personal annual appraisal: however, a major difference from New York is that the system is not all one way. The Area Commander can expect personal coaching and help to achieve the Area's objectives, and practical support and 'best practice' advice are available from the various Headquarters Consultancy Departments.

The issue of accountability leads us back to the second key question. What are the implications for the overall style of policing introduced by the NYPD reforms; and is improvement sustainable for the longer term?

What are the Policing Implications for the Future?

Whilst some of the formal policies of NYPD are clearly aimed at community policing, the rhetoric behind the changes does not match up with the deeds. I have already described the emphasis on enforcement and aggressive policing; of confrontational accountability systems; and the over-emphasis on quantitative statistical measures without compensating qualitative data. No matter how far the written policies talk about community policing, if the values and systems of the organisation do not support it—or worse, as appears to be the case in NYPD, they actually conflict with it—then a community style of policing is doomed to failure.

The consequences of that could be serious. Firstly, although strong enforcement tactics obtain good results in the early stages—as they clearly have in New York—there comes a time when those sections of the community who feel they bear the brunt will become alienated from the police. Law enforcement on its own has only limited capacity to deal with crime, disorder and fear. One can go so far in applying 'Zero Tolerance' but the time will come when it is not enough, and it is seen not to be enough. Then 'Zero Tolerance' will become positively counter-productive.

It may then be too late. Firstly, the police will have lost touch with the community. Confidence will have drained away. Tensions will have risen. It will then need only a spark to ignite serious disorder, as happened in Los Angeles following the Rodney King case. We know about these things in England too.

They happened in our own inner cities in the 1980s, and we have learned hard lessons of our own.[6]

Secondly, the culture of the organisation is all important to the values of individual police officers. If the pressure for results brings dubious practices in the recording of crime, what is the next stage? Similar problems will spread to other aspects of policing. It will spill over into the way in which police officers regard and treat the community. In the words of a New York Police Sergeant: 'They're yelling and pointing fingers at me at Headquarters. I come back and yell and point fingers at my people. They then go on the streets and do the same thing'.

But it will probably go further than that. It will lead inexorably to the falsifying of evidence in court. Corruption will start, and it could spread like a cancer through the organisation. It is not a question of 'if', but rather a question of 'when'.

This, then, is the challenge facing New York for the future. If the NYPD is to sustain its improvement—and if it is to avoid the risk of community disorder and of internal corruption—it will need to look carefully at its organisational culture, at its style and its methods of working. If the police on their own seek to take the credit now for reductions in crime—if they use the terminology 'I' or 'we the police' rather than 'we the police working with our communities'—so they will be the ones to attract the blame if it all goes wrong.

I now turn to consider what we in the UK can learn from the experience of 'Zero Tolerance'; but to do that it is necessary first to contrast policing in New York with that of the UK.

The Distinctions Between Policing in New York and the UK

The first and most significant difference is the environment in which policing takes place. This is of course very different in the US, quite apart from the special conditions of New York. Not only are social problems on a different scale but the whole nature of policing is skewed by the availability and legality of firearms. Thus the inner city problems of crime and disorder in the large urban conurbations are even more deep-seated than our own; and the propensity for violent crime—and fear of crime—is on a completely different scale.

As we have seen, the problems facing New York in 1994 were even bigger than that. By way of example, in comparison with London (a city of similar size), New York had nine times as many murders;[7] and twice as many rapes and robberies.[8] The feeling of vulnerability and insecurity of New York's citizens was justifiably high.

In terms of policing resources too, New York had many more police officers available than London. That was so even before New York gained a further 7,000 officers in the early 1990s. At the time Bratton took over, of the UK forces only the Royal Ulster Constabulary—a force faced with policing a community in a state of virtual civil war—had a similar ratio of police officers to population (1 : 200). The Metropolitan Police have one officer to every 253 members of the population.[9] Further afield, in Thames Valley we have one officer for every 533 members of the population. Remember too that UK police forces carry out the extra roles provided in the US by a plethora of other agencies such as the FBI, DEA, ATF, Secret Service and others. So these are huge variations in the ratio of police to population. Clearly there is a direct link between the intensity of resources available to police commanders and the efficacy of the policing solutions they implement, whatever style of policing they adopt.

The other fundamental difference between US and English policing is in tradition. Perhaps the clearest reflection of this is that if one speaks to US police officers, they will often describe themselves as being 'in law enforcement', in contrast to the traditional UK view of police as 'keepers of the peace'. The idea of the 'Sovereign's peace' can be traced back to the days of King Alfred and the preservation of the peace has been the task both of communities and of police to this day.

The most succinct statement of what community policing means in the 1990s is provided by the Operational Policing Review:

> British traditional policing is relatively low on numbers, low on power and high on accountability; it is undertaken with public consent which does not mean acquiescence but a broad tolerance indicating a satisfaction with both the helping and enforcement roles of policing. Its structure allows the public to express their policing wants and needs and through changes in social attitudes and methods of social control may occur, the culture of policing remains intact.

That culture is epitomised by the single constable, close to the community, patrolling the beat with the consent of the general public, armed only with lawful powers and the use of discretion.[10]

Although we in Britain went through the 'professional era' as described by Bratton—more officers taking to cars, more remote computerised command and control systems—the local touch never disappeared.

Lest British police officers should feel too superior, we should be aware that it is our transatlantic cousins who have provided most of the innovative thinking about community policing over the last two decades. It was Kelling and Wilson, as we have seen, who developed the ideas behind 'Broken Windows' around the fictitious community beat officer 'Kelly' in Newark, New Jersey in 1982; and Professor Herman Goldstein, from Madison, Wisconsin, is the 'father' of problem-oriented policing which is now rapidly gaining currency in the US, and to some extent in the UK. It is therefore somewhat ironic that the concept of 'Zero Tolerance'—which has little of the depth and integrity of either of these two philosophies—should be the one that has created the current media debate about policing.

The significance of our different policing traditions is that, in a limited sense, 'Zero Tolerance' has always been part of the English policing tradition. As we have seen above, 'Zero Tolerance' in New York suggests tackling low-level disorder and incivilities, albeit through a narrow, aggressive and uncompromising law enforcement approach. Tackling 'broken windows' is something that has always happened in English policing: it is just that we use a different way of explaining it. In England it is enshrined in the concept of 'the Bobby on the Beat'.

Why is it that everyone wants to see their local 'Bobby'? It is precisely because they deal with the incivilities, the low-level disorder and vandalism that undermine quality of life. Citizens feel reassured when they see him or her on foot patrol because they sense that things are in control, that incivilities will be dealt with effectively and streets kept safe. They sense that their presence, with sufficient numbers and regularity, will help reduce the likelihood of crime.

What they do not want to see, however, is police officers who feel no allegiance to their community, who appear to have no discretion about arresting or prosecuting offenders, and whose

'Zero Tolerance' attitude is dictatorial, inflexible and oppressive. It is these very features which, when they have occurred in British policing history (for example, in the 1980s), have alienated the community and resulted in corruption and riots.

In fact the 'Bobby on the Beat' has this last year been a media story too; but no-one has connected the issue with 'Zero Tolerance'. It has been of media interest because of the constant demand by the public for more police officers to be provided by government for visible police patrol, reflected in the commitments of both main political parties to increase the policing budget. It is a constant theme in the minds of Chief Constables as they struggle to balance the demand for policing among the many pressures they face. And it is reflected in the debate generated by the recent Audit Commission publication 'Streetwise',[11] which dealt with the whole issue of the 'Bobbies on the Beat', why they are so important and the effectiveness of their deployment.

The key to understanding the links between 'Bobbies on the Beat' and 'Zero Tolerance' is to analyse what happened in New York. 'Zero Tolerance' probably did play a part in a reduction in crime, in the sense that what had presumably been allowed to occur on the streets, in terms of incivilities and disorder, was very serious and needed to be addressed. Indeed the lack of control of the streets was at crisis point, markedly more serious than any comparable situation in the UK, even taking account of our most difficult inner city areas. When Bratton applied basic management principles to shake up the NYPD, therefore, the scope to make improvements out on the streets was huge and excellent results thankfully—and perhaps inevitably—occurred.

But two things must not be forgotten. Firstly, Bratton had at his disposal a huge number of police officers. The problem of the past was that they had not been motivated or directed in any kind of co-ordinated way, so the fact of utilising them much more effectively brought the desired result. But it is important to get this in perspective. An extra 7,000 police officers is an enormous number: I wonder what the Metropolitan Police in London would achieve with 7,000 extra Bobbies patrolling the streets of London. Similarly in Thames Valley, a proportionate increase of 870 extra officers on top of our existing 3,800 would provide enormous potential to increase public safety and reduce crime much further than we have already achieved—almost beyond my wildest imagination!

The second point is that any improvements, particularly on such a peak of high crime and disorder, are likely to be governed by the law of diminishing returns. A powerful injection of staff, motivation and direction is bound to have a positive impact in the early stages, but as things improve so it becomes more and more difficult to achieve further gains. For police forces seeking improvements from a much lower base of crime and disorder (as in the UK), with few extra resources, the potential is obviously far more limited.

Conclusion

The conclusions to be drawn from my analysis of 'Zero Tolerance' in New York are threefold.

Firstly, William Bratton is to be congratulated on what he achieved in New York. Whilst there are doubts about how far his policy of 'Zero Tolerance' contributed to the reductions in crime and disorderly behaviour, there is no doubt that his inspirational leadership had a direct impact on the NYPD and, through that, the safety and quality of life of New Yorkers.

But the reasons behind the improvements are complex. Policing was only one of numerous variable factors affecting crime levels in New York; and Bratton had vast resources with which to do it. That is not to take anything away from him for shaking up an organisation clearly in need of strong leadership. But it does raise the question of whether 'Zero Tolerance' itself was a key factor, or indeed a factor at all. The improved management, motivation and accountability of such a large number of police officers may well have brought these results regardless of which policing style was adopted.

Bratton should also be congratulated on creating the media debate about 'Zero Tolerance'. Whilst it is a very imprecise term with different meanings for different people, it has focused the public imagination on an important aspect of policing. In particular, it does no harm to remind police officers in the UK of the rationale behind the Bobby on the Beat, and the importance of dealing effectively with low-level incivilities and disorder.

Secondly, whilst Bratton and the NYPD responded well to the crisis of confidence afflicting policing in New York, there are huge challenges for the future. This for me is the most significant issue of the whole debate. The success so far has achieved powerful short-term results, and this has brought time and space to develop complementary, community-based strategies for the future. In fact, the reforms carried out so far may be as nothing compared to the reforms needed now to keep the NYPD working closely in harmony with its community.

That part of the 'Zero Tolerance' principle characterised by aggressive policing, confrontational management, opportunistic short-termism and undue emphasis on 'the numbers game' poses an enormous threat to the future. If this culture is not tackled, then—on the basis of the British experience—the risk of serious corruption and inner-city disorder in the future is real.

Finally, the analysis of 'Zero Tolerance' confirms my thesis at the beginning of this paper. Of the different styles of policing being applied by Police Departments in the United States, it is the 'problem-oriented policing' approach like that in San Diego which has most to offer in terms of an enduring, long-term approach to improving community safety. Indeed with limited resources and ever-increasing demands upon us, it is the only one that police leaders can pursue with confidence for the future.

That is why we in Thames Valley will continue to develop 'problem-solving policing' with determination, innovation and vision. Identifying and tackling the root causes of crime, disorder and fear in conjunction with our partners in the community, rather than repeatedly and superficially treating the symptoms, is the best way of policing as we move into the next Millennium.

Confident Policing
in Hartlepool

Norman Dennis and Ray Mallon

THIS CHAPTER and the next are an attempt to set policing in a particular context within which it had to work, and to assess the impact that policing, as a specialized and limited social function, could make and did make as the context changed.

They are a combined effort. The specialist contribution from the sociologist in some parts will be as obvious to the reader as the specialist contribution of the policeman in others. But elsewhere in the mixture of our ideas, experiences and interpretations our contributions will be indistinguishable, especially as we describe and reflect upon Hartlepool itself, a town local to us both as County Durham men.[1]

In Hartlepool there are no big-time criminals. Serious crimes are rare. Weapons, for example, are seldom used—by American standards or the standards now of the English big city.[2] Three recent criminal cases attracting nation-wide attention were the murder of a child by a paedophile, and the death of 77-year-old who disturbed a youth attempting to steal his motor car from his home. The thief reversed at speed and killed him.[3] In December 1994 a 16-year-old Hartlepool youth was killed by the dangerous driving of a 21-year-old car thief, who received a five-year sentence. A year later indignation was still high, when a 25,000-name petition was handed to the town's MP calling for heavier sentences for such crimes.[4] In this town of 90,000 a total of 12,800 crimes were recorded by the police in the year March 1995 to April 1996.[5]

But given the relative pettiness of its normal crimes and disorder, from small beginnings their growth, as in New York, has been steep since the mid-1950s, and especially from the

1970s, until pulled back by police action and other focused anti-crime measures in the mid-1990s. The police's failed and successful initiatives have been surprisingly similar in the two places both in content and timing, to such an extent that William J. Bratton, the New York police commissioner (1994-1996), thought it worth while to pay a visit to Hartlepool to examine the police work there.

Coincident with changed police strategy and tactics, crime in both New York City, Hartlepool and in other places was cut in the 1990s.

According to police figures, in New York serious crime dropped by 27 per cent from 1993 to 1995. In 1995 there were 35,400 street robberies; in 1996 there were 30,400. The record of 2,200 murders was set in 1990. In 1996 the total was under 1,000 for the first time since 1968.[6]

Hartlepool's crime figures were also cut. Comparing 1994 with 1996, the total of reported crimes was down by 27 per cent, from 15,600 to 11,300.[7] The volume crimes that most directly and seriously impact upon the lives of individuals in a place like Hartlepool are domestic burglary and car crimes. Thefts of vehicles were down by 56 per cent.[8] Domestic burglaries were down by 31 per cent.[9] Thefts from vehicles were down by 15 per cent.[10]

The seriousness of the rate of growth of crime which the town had experienced in the years preceding 1994 is shown by the fact that even these dramatic successes had driven recorded crime in some monthly periods only back down to the levels recorded in 1991.[11]

The police are to some extent in control of their own strategy and tactics; but they are to some extent in control (or potentially in control) of the indices of their own success also, namely, the figures of recorded crime. It is therefore essential to present an account that is sufficiently full for the reader to make his or her own assessment of whether crime did rise in Hartlepool, and whether it was reduced in the 1990s. If crime did rise and fall, the reader must be enabled to make his or her own best judgement on the most reasonable, if provisional, explanation on the basis of the best data available. After two years' experience of it, the local journalists, certainly, were quite convinced of the success of the crime strategy.

Anyone living in the town in the last two years cannot have failed to notice the no-nonsense detective, nor ignore the spectacular results he and his team have notched up. His unique crime-beating strategy has cut crime levels in Hartlepool ... by a massive 30-per-cent-plus ... with the number of recorded burglaries in July looking to make a record breaking plummet to less than 100. In a town where house burglaries once topped 300 a month, it's a statistic to be proud of.[12]

The Rise in Crime

The figures for the Hartlepool Division of Cleveland Constabulary are not always separately available in the Chief Constable's Annual Reports (which date from 1983) but the trend of the Hartlepool figures, when they are given, is in line with that of the whole Cleveland Constabulary area.

Between 1980 and 1992, in a period of only twelve years, the crime figures for Cleveland County more than doubled, and in 1992 *in Cleveland County alone there was almost exactly the same number of crimes recorded as had been recorded in the whole of England and Wales ninety years before*—80,000 in Cleveland County in 1992 as compared with 81,000 in England and Wales in 1901.

There were more than *three times* as many burglaries in 1992 than there had been only twelve years before. (In 1980 there were 4,300 recorded cases of house burglary in the Cleveland County police area. By 1992 there were 13,200.) In nine of the eleven years 1983-94 the crime rate rose year-on-year, the highest rises being 22 per cent, 14 per cent and 12 per cent. The rate fell only twice, and by much lower percentages, seven per cent and three per cent.[13]

In the four months before Ray Mallon took over as chief of crime strategy at Hartlepool the monthly crime figure had risen by 38 per cent (to 1,600 cases). Burglary had risen by 31 per cent.

Hartlepool spends half of its bus-shelter maintenance budget on repairing the results of deliberate destruction.[14]

In 1996 Cleveland Fire Brigade was offered a government loan for a 'community education programme' because of the growing number of malicious false alarms. There were over 500 more false emergency calls in 1996 than there had been in 1995. (This brought the total to more than 3,300.)[15]

Near certain residential areas of the town, acts of sheer destruction as well as crimes for gain in some of the new industrial areas were a weighty disincentive to firms making decisions about coming to or remaining in Hartlepool.

Some firms in the Jutland Road area, for example, simply gave up in defeat. They found facilities smashed up as soon as they were installed. In other industrial areas, such as the Graythorp Industrial Estate, after a period of defeatism during which firms ceased to report the seemingly endless incidents and then pulled out, the users organized their own security patrols and introduced other pooled measures to combat vandalism and theft. By the mid-1990s, every new development in the town, domestic, commercial or industrial, was scrutinized from the point of view of its crime-prevention potentialities.

Hartlepool is one of a handful of local authorities selected nationally for the so-called 'One Stop Shop Initiative', and at a weekly meeting of the various agencies and authorities concerned with development applications, the police representative gives a view on the security aspects of residential and industrial proposals.

Confident Policing

When we turn to the period when strategy and tactics in Hartlepool were heavily stamped with the influence of what we have termed 'confident policing', it is inappropriate for the detective chief inspector personally involved to be the reporter. The account of it that follows is therefore that of Norman Dennis, who has studied the evidence to the best of his ability as an objective observer. 'Objectivity' in social research means nothing more (or less) than self-consciousness about, and reining in, one's own pre-conceptions and preferences, and using the methods of sociology, methods that are mainly designed to reduce as far as possible the distortions that personal hopes and fears intrude into both perception and description. (That effort is all that is 'scientific' about 'social science'.)

Ray Mallon took up his appointment as the new head of crime strategy for the Hartlepool division on 18 April 1994.

A principal role in its own right for any police force, of course, is the detection of crimes and the apprehension of suspects. But he believed that two roles at least as important had been losing the prominence they deserved.

One was *reducing* the number of crimes to the extent that this was within the scope of British policing methods. The second was retaining or recovering the control of the streets on behalf and with the consent of the law-abiding population, again, in the British tradition of give-and-take and with all allowance for harmless high spirits, with tolerance of mere eccentricity, and with all compassion for personality disorders.

The police force in Hartlepool would tackle these objectives by simply paying attention to, not ignoring, anti-social behaviour and 'nuisance crime'. The effective control of the situation is rarely secured by 'zero tolerance' in the sense of an intolerant and over-bearing demeanour. British police practice has always recognized the empirical importance, in controlling the situation, of preventing the escalation of the problem. All that zero tolerance meant in Hartlepool, within the specific cultural history of working class citizenship there, and the specific legal framework, rules and traditions of the policing, was that the police would 'return peace to the streets' by controlling minor situations in the interest of the 'decent' and 'respectable' citizen.

Implicit in this strategy, though not always articulated, was the assumption that the idea of the 'decent' and 'respectable' citizen was not an absurdity exposed and exploded by enlightened students, social workers, philosophers, agony aunts, and other proponents of post-modernism. It was to be fundamental to police work in Hartlepool. If a police officer was acting on behalf of the decent, law-abiding citizens of the town, within the law and according to good British police practice, then he or she was doing a proper job. Because the Hartlepool division of Cleveland constabulary was small, and the police officers were principally drawn from the respectable elements of the local working-class community, this was not a difficult assumption for them to work with. In Hartlepool, benefiting in that sense from being somewhat off the track beaten by fashionable intellectuals, it was still largely taken for granted by them.

A central intention of the strategy in Hartlepool was to break into the vicious spiral of a deteriorating situation of personal safety, defacement and dereliction on the streets; a reduction in the law-abiding citizen's confidence in his own capacity and the capacity of the police to control the situation; a further deterioration as the confidence of the unruly elements increases; and a further loss of public confidence in itself and the police.

'Keeping an Eye on Things'

The fear generated by law-breaking was to be lifted from the law-abiding citizen. One of the means by which this was be accomplished was the removal of anonymity from delinquents and gang members. Police officers come simply to know them—and make it clear that they know they know them. Hartlepool is the type of place where this is still feasible. Another means, whenever appropriate and likely to be effective, is not to ignore deliberate, even if petty, individual demonstrations of disrespect to and defiance of the police officer, like an adolescent continuing in his presence to ride a bicycle along the pavement or in the dark without lights. The police officer does not arrest the ten-year-old who is swearing. But he or she gets out the police car and 'pays attention' to the event, face-to-face.

There is a Greek myth about a man called Gyges who went into a cave and found a ring that had the power to turn him invisible. He used his invisibility to evade the guards at the palace and seduce the queen. He used it to poison the king so that he and the queen could marry. He used it as king to commit in secret every atrocious crime against his subjects that he thought would be of advantage to himself. Plato used 'the ring of Gyges' as the test of a person's true virtue. 'Would you act in that criminal or immoral way if you knew for certain nobody would ever know it was you?' His point was that in real life even the most virtuous people need some fear of exposure and scandal, if they are to give due weight to the interests of other people when those interests clash with their own—'due' weight in practice being defined by the law or by customary views about what is 'fair', 'decent', 'right', with the law and custom often being in close agreement.

One of the sources of angry frustration in the town was that victims often knew only too well who the perpetrators of crimes and quality-of-life offences against them were—and that they and 'the authorities' seemed quite incapable of bringing them to book. But DCI Mallon saw that an essential element in growing crime had been this aspect of 'the breakdown of community': anti-social elements were far less likely than in the past to be known to the people against whom they were offending. This was, of course, very marked in the big cities. But it applied in measure to small towns like Hartlepool too. Knowledge that the offence had been committed by *him*, that known boy, was decreasingly likely to feed back to anyone who had any control over him.

Modern society had, so to speak, handed to every boy the ring of Gyges.

The first thing to do, therefore, was to take it away from him. Confident policing of low-order offences involves at its mildest—but also at its very effective—simply letting the boy or the young man know that if he pushes high spirits into intimidation, if he spray paints the bus seats, if he sniffs glue under the old railway bridge, if he smashes the seat in the park, the chances have been considerably raised that someone will effectively know that *he* was the culprit.

In order to give police officers the local focus that is necessary if they are to be seen 'keeping an eye on things' in this way, teams were organized, each responsible for its own problem housing estate. This is not the eye of Big Brother on behalf of the party. That is a typical exaggeration and misleading analogy beloved of anti-police pressure groups. It is a benevolent eye on behalf of ordinary people.

Orwell's nightmare of Big Brother emerged out the absence of English-type law and order, not out of its existence, as any Jew from Nazi Germany and any 'enemy of the people' from Communist Hungary would testify. This is a point George Erdos, a patriotic Englishman who has had deep personal experience of all three, strongly urges in *Families Without Fatherhood*.[16]

In 1995-96 these teams dealt formally with 59 cases of boys and young men hanging about shopping precincts, intimidating residents and passers-by. Thirty-one of the cases were dealt with merely by sending a letter to the youngster's parents saying what he had been doing. In 28 cases the youngster was arrested.[17]

The definition of how far it is 'reasonable in all the circumstances' to relax the law is a decision for the police to make, within the guidelines laid down or accepted by senior officers, the civil authorities, and public opinion, with the policeman's exercise of discretion being subject to subsequent sanctions if abusively heavy-handed or unwisely lenient. The discretion of what laws are 'reasonable', and what degree of relaxation in their observance is 'appropriate in all the circumstances', is not to be exercised by any particular private individual according to his own view of the matter at the time.

Hanging about in a verbally abusive gang, urinating in the lift, smashing the lights on the footpath, spraying graffiti on a house wall, smashing a seat in the park, are the starting points of a criminal career. As DCI Mallon said, 'Boys and young men don't go straight from being cheeky to their parents into burglary—any more than children go straight from the primary school into the university'. Police action at this level therefore can have the effect in some cases of closing the criminal-career path early. In the mid-1950s the police operated on the assumption that the best way to keep crime down was to intervene early and confidently. Crime rates were low, and the number of children picked up by the police declined as the children matured into their teens. By the mid-1990s, by contrast, the number picked up by the police nationally roughly tripled from their early teens to their late teens.[18]

Another spin-off from paying attention to minor offences envisaged by this crime strategy was that it could lead to the detection of other offences and suspects.

Targeting the Burglar

One focus of Hartlepool's new crime strategy, therefore, was on this confident policing of minor offences and sub-criminal disorder. The other focus was on house burglary. From the point of view of the victim, worse things can happen even in Hartlepool as a result of criminal activity. But to have one's house broken into is, in the normal course of things, one of the main components in 'the fear of crime' in the town.

House burglars are by no means top of the criminal pecking order in big cities like New York or Glasgow. But in a small town like Hartlepool they are. The house burglar is the most determined of all those who contribute to the figures of *volume* crime. A burglary is an extremely difficult offence to complete. The burglar has to find the likely house; break into it; get the stolen property out; and then get rid of it. If burglars can boast of success, then they can influence by their example other boys whose feet are not yet on the criminal ladder.

House burglars are not opportunists. It is on their mind to find a house to break into. They are on the lookout for weak targets. But if they find a still weaker one, they will take advantage of that. They will steal 'anything that isn't nailed down'. If the police can restrain the house burglar, therefore, all the other offences he would normally have committed are reduced as well.

Burglary has this additional feature. By the 1990s, as a matter of empirical fact, the only volume-crime offender normally sent to prison was the convicted burglar. If he is caught and convicted, therefore, he is put completely out of circulation. About two-thirds of crime is committed by one-fifth of offenders. Home Office research suggests that nationally the number of burglaries committed by offenders while serving community service sentences ranged between three and thirteen. These could have been prevented if the burglars had been sent to prison for a year instead.[19] This is where, in the sense of the phrase as it was popularized by the Home Secretary, Michael Howard, 'jail works'. It makes it physically impossible for the burglar to be either breaking into houses or committing any of the other offences for which he would have been responsible if he had been at large.

The basis of this aspect of the strategy was, therefore, that *in a place like Hartlepool* policing the burglar could have a considerable limiting effect on all criminal activity in the town. The number of burglars makes the problem, so to speak, 'manageable'. At any one time there is a hard-core of only perhaps thirty or so. Targeting the burglar could be effective in the short term, by putting him out of business. It could be effective also in the longer term, by making him into a failure instead of a success and therefore undermining his position as a principal role-model for young criminals or would-be criminals. 'The main players in the criminal fraternity are being taken out of the game because we are targeting them at every opportunity.'[20]

'Targeting', and in particular targeting the serial robber and burglar, was being simultaneously adopted elsewhere. In the Blyth Valley police area of Northumbria Constabulary, for example (Blyth itself is very similar to Hartlepool in size and industrial and social history), robberies dropped from 97 in 1995 to 59 in 1996, a fall of nearly 40 per cent. House burglaries dropped from 2,800 to 2,200, a fall of over 20 per cent. The commanding officer, Superintendent Alan Pape, said: 'We have information on what they are doing. We follow them from their homes until we catch them red-handed committing a crime'. In the Northumbria Constabulary area as a whole, the reported crime figure in 1996 was a third lower than the figure in 1991, the longest run of consecutive falls of any force in the country.[21]

The tactics in Hartlepool included the cultivation of informants, and generally encouraging information-based police action. With rising confidence in the police, the public became much more forthcoming. (Alan Pape at Blyth said that there, there had been an 'overwhelming' rise in tip-offs from the public.)[22] Constables fed back their own direct knowledge from their patrols. 'Crime happens in the community, not in the police station.'

The British policeman has the legal right to stop and 'interact' with anyone. If he has reasonable grounds for suspicion he can search him. Public hostility severely hinders police work, and 'stop' and 'stop and search' powers must be used with the utmost care. But in a town like Hartlepool, they can be more effectively concentrated on known malefactors going about their business at suspicious times or in suspicious circumstances with a surer touch than they can in the big city.

Winning within the Rules—But Winning

However, if this strategy were to be effectively carried out, and these tactics properly applied within the law and the customs and experience of British policing, the success of the strategy aimed at the Hartlepool police force itself was an essential prerequisite. Since the cultural revolution of the 1960s police officers had inevitably also been influenced by the idea that the real causes of crime were economic, and crime could only be tackled by attacking the 'root causes'. With the expansion of university departments of social work and social policy, and with the vastly increased numbers of students influenced by 'critical social theory' and 'the new criminology' in their university, polytechnic, Open University, further education and professional or semi-professional courses, this idea became the staple of the serious media, and gradually consensual in the whole of British society. An associated idea was that no action relating to crime or criminals was truly appropriate except social-work type treatment.

The results of forty years of knocking away the intellectual props of police work—a process dealt with in the Editor's Introduction—had worked themselves down into every police station in Britain. The first thing that Ray Mallon did, therefore, was to attack the attitude that the police could not do very much, and perhaps were not entitled to do very much, to affect the volume of crime; the idea that crime was really caused by the massive 'bad environment' and 'deprivation' out there, which 'the government' was too malign or too mean to change.

On first taking up his appointment, Ray Mallon had called together officers of all ranks, to inform them that tolerance and give-and-take whenever possible, but minimal robustness whenever necessary, within the law and the traditions of consensual English policing, could make inroads only so far into crime and disorder, but that inroads *could* be made.

The magnitude of police effectiveness he put in the region of a 20 per cent cut in crime. This figure was based upon his previous experience in the police division of Cleveland Constabulary from which he had been transferred to take up the post at Hartlepool, initially as head of the CID.

Before Tony Blair had announced, as Leader of the Labour Party, that the country needed three things, education, education and education, Ray Mallon was driving home the message that the three things he regarded as most important for successful policing were attitude, attitude, attitude. A central feature of his work, therefore, was to promote 'the clear message that the business of the Hartlepool police is to reduce crime through a programme of positive policing' at meetings that all available ranks were required to attend.[23]

Ray Mallon, as chief of crime strategy at Hartlepool, regarded it as essential that police officers should have their confidence restored in both the legitimacy and the efficacy of their limited and specific *policing* role. 'Morale is everything.' From the first day of his appointment, he set out to convince Hartlepool division that while they could not get at many of the other 'root causes' of crime, they could get at one of them, the 'root cause' that policing had become less effective than it could be. 'You *can* make a difference.' Not only could they become more effective. What they were doing was worthwhile. 'We are the good-doers. Assert that, don't deny it. That is what we are. Other people who claim to be do-gooders might be or might not be, but we are real good-doers.'

'"We want more resources!" Yes, we want more resources. But for fifteen years we have soaked up "resources" like a sponge, and we haven't been able to show ourselves or anybody else what we are producing with them.'

I was thoroughly sick of police officers who said, 'We can't do it'. It is like a footballer who says, 'we can't score any goals'. Of course he won't score any, and he won't help the team. It is better to have one police officer who is positive, than two who are defeatist. A defeatist policeman is not simply a burden of one on his own. Negativity is like an infectious disease. There is little negativity in Hartlepool. In the parade room the Chief Inspector in charge of the uniformed officers tells those with ten years service and those with just three months service, 'Get out there. When you have to be, be aggressive in a controlled way. We can do it'.

In his approach to the 'hearts and minds' of the workforce itself, Ray Mallon modelled himself on sports' team management and leadership on the field. He was a great admirer of Peter Reid, the manager of Sunderland AFC. Reid is determined and passionate—and does not like losing. He had taken over a squad which was deficient in footballers of the individual calibre playing for, say, Middlesbrough or Newcastle. But by good man-management and good organization on the field, he had produced a successful Premier League team of whole-hearted, determined and well-organized players.

He asked questions and listened to the answers given by other senior officers.

'Why is crime going through the roof?'

'Would you like to tell me what you think we can do about it?'

The size and character of the Hartlepool division made it a comparatively favourable environment within which both good man-management and good team tactics could succeed. Because of the small numbers of police and civilian staff, the crime-strategy chief could interact directly and daily with the Commander of Hartlepool District, to whom he was directly answerable, and with the heads of the CID, the uniformed officers and the specialized support services. Of course, they had to be willing and able to work amicably together, and sort out any differences between themselves satisfactorily. The personalities, skills and commitment of all of them, as it turned out, were equal to the task. This essential element in success cannot always be replicated.

The personnel of the district comprised the District Commander, and under him three Chief Inspectors. One was the CI in charge of Crime Management and Crime Strategy. The second CI was in charge of Operations. He was responsible for seeing that the crime strategy was implemented. Under him were nine

Inspectors, namely, one for each shift of the four-shift twenty-four hours; one for each of the four areas into which Hartlepool was divided for the purposes of community police-team work; and the Detective Inspector in charge of the CID, the most important section of which was the Operational Intelligence Branch, under a detective sergeant. The CID was composed of three detective sergeants and eighteen detective constables.

In addition to CID officers and support staff, at any one time about 12-18 police officers could be expected to be actually on duty in Hartlepool, some of them in cars, and some on foot. The third of the chief inspectors was in charge of the Personnel, Training and Welfare branch. In addition, there was a sergeant in charge of Community Affairs and a sergeant in charge of the Community Safety branch (each with five constables under—at that time—him).

What is more, on this scale the particular flavour of management could infuse the whole workforce. The particular flavour of management at Hartlepool was that of 'winning without cheating, winning *within the rules*'. Winning outside the rules rendered what one was doing not just unjust or unfair, but meaningless. As Ray Mallon put it:

> I come from a sporting background. From the age of 11 until I was 22 I swam four hours a day, six days a week. I played sport at high level until 23, as captain of the Great Britain under-20 water polo team, and then on the senior team. Don't cheat! You are only cheating yourself!

Team Work and Team Spirit

Supervising a small workforce, the driving-force of the operation could take a personal interest in the care of his subordinates—'treat people properly'. Ray Mallon says easily as a secretary comes up to us, and in her presence, 'I recruited her. I will try to move her career along. Civilians are as important as police officers.'

Some organizational structures are too large to be amenable to anything but quite exceptional charismatic leadership. Some organizational structures are on a scale small enough to make leadership possible, but lack the necessary charismatic leader.

In Hartlepool, from 1994 to 1996 (at least), there was a small homogeneous team, prepared by the previous leadership, *and* an innovative leader, whose style and achievements could be built on by his successors.

It always has to be remembered that a 'policy' on the ground depends upon the personnel who operate it, and the spirit in which they do it. It can easily be imagined that 'zero-tolerance' policing (especially with that title) could drift into ham-fisted bullying were it not kept under constant surveillance, or into 'going through the motions' in an over-large, over-bureaucratized organization. An essential element in the Hartlepool situation was the fact that there was no friction at all between Ray Mallon and the three successive Commanders of the Hartlepool division, Terry Romeanes, Paul Garvin and Christine Twigg. Paul Garvin was Commander for most of the period, from September 1994 to April 1996, and he showed constant courage and determination in defending the innovative work being undertaken. 'He trusted my judgement. He backed me up.' For as long as Ray Mallon was there, there was 'never any light between me and any of the Commanders, whether Terry Romeanes, Paul Garvin or Superintendent Mrs. Twigg'. Where there is not this solidarity among senior officers, of course, the results can be expected to be different.

Because of the homogeneity of the background of most of his officers, from the same heavy industrial area of south Durham and Teesside, the problem was minimized of conscious, or more often unconscious, disparities in what is taken for granted as sensible and desirable over a host of matters and in all the nooks and crannies of decision-taking and consent.

Team-work, here as in any other business or game, depended on specialization on the one hand, and shared knowledge and co-ordination on the other.

Motivating the team, and sharing knowledge about the opponent, the role of each member, the current conditions, and the state of play, was fostered by Ray Mallon's reinforcing his message at weekly and other meetings. The intelligence branch of the Hartlepool division was put at the hub of operations. Around the hub, but interacting with each other, were the crime desk, receiving information and passing it to the intelligence branch for dissemination throughout the system, the uniform branch, the local beat officers (LBOs), CID, and the specialized field officers. As Ray Mallon said:

They all have to know their bit-parts. The importance of each role and of its part in the overall strategy is a message that has to be constantly reinforced. It is a matter of 'gelling' the different parts of the workforce.

Not surprisingly the book on management that most appeals to him is Mark H. McCormack's *The 110% Solution*,[24] for McCormack is one of his generation's great motivators of the world's top sportsmen. 'I have my officers read it. I sometimes quote paragraphs from McCormack at meetings to make a point.'

> You must get structure right [Mallon said]. You've got to get roles and responsibilities right. Each of the reliefs, each team, over the twenty-four hours has to be balanced and blended as a team. Each team needs someone good with informants. To be good with informants the officer has to have presence and personality—perhaps one in five of CID officers. You need someone who is dependable in carrying out basic tasks. If at all possible you want someone with flair. You try to find a couple for each team who have the basic skills, and who stick to the job—the hewers of wood and drawers of water. The best football teams are those that do all things right. They have mastered basic skills. They each know what the game-plan is. They patiently do all things competently. Within the structure and the basic skills, when the opening appears they succeed with flair. You keep the structure, shape, blend, even when things are going badly. A good manager is one who doesn't lose his nerve and the faith in his principles under the pressure of failure. The first week I got there I said: 'This is the strategy. It works. I won't change it. Stick to the strategy!'

During his 22 years' police service he had spent most of his time in the CID. 'But I had come from the uniform branch like everybody else. Some CID officers forget that they did too. I won't put up with that. I am pro-uniform, pro-CID, pro-police.' In his previous post, as a detective inspector at South Bank, Langbaugh (1989-1992), he had worked with uniformed police officers more than with other CID officers. His strategy there had contributed to the reduction of house burglaries by 33 per cent in two years. The lesson he had drawn from his South Bank years was that favourable results could be gained from closing the traditional gap between the two branches—especially by combating the *de haut en bas* attitude of the detectives. He is therefore an advocate of the equality of status and the harmonization of the work of the CID and of uniformed officers. Uniformed constables and CID officers patrolled together.

In detail, internal morale was also a matter of the good manners of colleagues in their relationships with one another. To say 'detail' is not to say 'unimportant'. As the German saying has it, 'The Devil is in the details'.

Involving the Citizenry

An effort to re-introduce the pervasive and unreflective (because taken for granted) sense of responsibility of all adults for maintaining decent and reasonable good order in their own street and locality, with due allowance for high spirits, individuality, and with a proper disdain for the interfering busybody and nosey parker, was a scheme introduced in 1995-96. In 'Ringmaster' the Hartlepool police, the participants in Neighbourhood Watch schemes, and representatives from the government-funded City Challenge exchanged messages through a shared computer network about, for example, where there had been spate of burglaries, or where there was a bogus caller or someone behaving in a suspicious manner.

As another way of restoring and symbolizing local civilian input into, confidence in, and responsibility for, the civil safety of their own communities, without the disorder of desperate 'end of our tether' vigilante movements, twenty new special constables were recruited in the two years during which DCI Mallon was head of crime strategy. The responsibility of all law-abiding citizens to maintain the conditions of their own freedom to go about their business within the framework approved by custom and permitted by law, without the fact and fear of unlawful disruption of it, was symbolized also by the co-operation of the Labour-controlled Borough Council in the recruitment of these 'specials'.[25]

The idea of the uniform covering not a martinet but just another civilian attending to the duties that lay on all citizens was a strong strand in the ideology, and therefore in the actuality, of English social control.

In a conversation Norman Dennis had reason to believe was frank, a middle-ranking police officer said to him:

> Ray Mallon took possession of the crime problem. Things changed dramatically. Everyone had been doing his best. But there was no strategy until Ray came. Now there are co-ordinated police teams instead of isolated beat officers. We are targeting the 'hard basket'. Burglary is the most difficult crime, so the burglar therefore finds no

difficulty and no motivational bar to committing lesser crimes. We disrupt his activities, and that stops his lesser crimes as well. Ray educated us. We didn't need much convincing. We had crime review meetings every Wednesday at 2 p.m. Ray insisted that every available officer was there—to be informed, to be told what was expected of us, and to give motivation speeches. That had not happened before. Football team? Absolutely! That was Ray's way of getting the message across. Historically there's been a gulf between uniform and CID. Ray created team harmony between us. The CID, and probably the rest of the police, were motivated by the commitment and drive of Ray Mallon. There is no need to bull him up. Everybody admires what he's done—police and public. House burglary and over-all crime have fallen month by month. It's worked. It's proved to be right. This *is* policing in Hartlepool District now.

A detective sergeant said of a particular incident: 'This is a typical example of Hartlepool police at work. It's not just the front line that tackles crime. We all have the same philosophy and we all do our bit.'[26]

Public Confidence in the Police

Ideally, of course, a social survey would have been carried out at least before the arrival of Ray Mallon in the Hartlepool Division and after he had left to give a more reliable indication of the character and distribution of different opinions and shades of opinion. But in the absence of such sample-survey data we must do with what we have. Norman Dennis entered into casual conversation with Hartlepudlians in order to raise the topic of the Mallon régime. There were a few sceptics who denied that crime had fallen, especially when they had a recent tale to tell of themselves or their acquaintances having been victims. But the vast majority said they felt safer and that this was the result of the new crime strategy.

Whatever the figures, what people thought about crime, their fear of crime, and what they thought about police effectiveness on their behalf, were important considerations in Hartlepool's crime strategy. The strategy was aimed not just at the law-breaker or the social nuisance, not just at the workforce, but at public opinion. Public opinion was also a place in the old vicious spiral that could be broken into with beneficial effects on the other phases. Ray Mallon's appointment was timely from this point of view. The public was ready to be convinced by him that the police ought to and could do something about criminals in Hartlepool. The public and politicians were up in arms. What are the police doing about it? He had been asked by the Assistant Chief Constable Ken Horner: 'Can you reduce crime?' He believed he could, by breaking into the vicious spiral at any point to turn it into a virtuous one. Improved performance by police leads to increased public confidence in the police. That leads to increased public support for the police. That feeds back into improved performance by police.

On 19 April 1994, the day after he took up his appointment, he approached the local newspapers and said that the police had become too satisfied that what they were doing was as much as they could do; in that sense they had become complacent. He said: 'We shall reduce crime. It we don't reduce it within twelve months, I'll ask to be removed as Detective Chief Inspector.'

'I soon concluded that public opinion was a crucial matter. I decided to go to media at every opportunity. I will talk to them at a moment's notice.'

An inspection of the file shows the local press coming round week by week to his point of view. At first he is the 'controversial' DCI, then the 'outspoken' DCI and finally and permanently the 'popular' DCI. William J. Bratton was Commissioner of the New York Police Department for only 27 months. There was some question that his popularity with the public had made him less than popular in other circles. Making this point, the local press said that 'luckily for Hartlepool, DCI Mallon is still in place', with the support of his then commander, Superintendent Christine Twigg, and his colleague Chief Inspector Dave Nixon.[27] Typical headlines by mid-1996 were: 'Crooks send him hate mail but public think he's great',[28] or 'Detective more than a match for yobs'.[29]

The printed and electronic media, that had previously looked to 'experts' from the local polytechnics or universities to interpret and comment on crime and police activities—which they had been doing according to the world-view stemming from the student movements of the 1960s—now printed and broadcast more easily the world-view underlying the Hartlepool police strategy. From undermining confidence in the police and sympathy for the victim, the new messages reinforced both.

Ray Mallon commented on the incongruence between what the police were doing and what the courts were doing. He saw his 'profit margin', his 'goal tally', as being tied up with the disposal of the suspects the police brought into the judicial system. 'It's like a football team getting in front of the goal—and the ball is knocked over the bar.'[30] Rhetorically addressing the magistrates and the judges, he said: 'My "profit" is the reduction in incidents of criminal activity. The police are protecting the law-abiding public. You are failing to do so. You are letting the public down every day. "Innocent unless proven guilty beyond reasonable doubt" is a great and precious rule. But we have the problem of how *those found guilty* are treated by the courts.' He used both the media and public meetings to put this message across. 'I have nothing to worry about. What I say is true. I can back it up with facts.'

It is not unlikely that he impacted on general Labour party thinking on crime from mid-1995. Peter Mandelson, the local MP influential in the inner councils of the Labour party, was present at a public meeting at the Hartlepool civic centre attended by 150 people as part of an anti-joyriding campaign. Ray Mallon told the audience that it was time for people to 'stand up and be counted'. He said that the ordinary 16- or 17-year-old criminal did not care about anybody else. 'He'd sell his own grandmother for a shilling.' But he was a coward who would run if he thought that there was a chance that he would be locked up. The police were doing their job within the rules. The magistrates were not doing theirs.

A senior magistrate said that the remarks were 'unbalanced'. Perhaps missing the point about sentencing, and the essential underlying trend that between 1954 and 1994 the odds of a convicted criminal being sent to prison had fallen by 80 per cent,[31] he concentrated on the separate question of the fairness of any guilty verdict and said that magistrates 'listen to the prosecution and defence, and then come up with a decision'.

But DCI Mallon's speech met with widespread public approval.[32] 'Fed-up residents are giving their full support to the town's top detective after reading about his controversial views on the legal system.'

> The town's population is singing his praises. 'He has spoken for the town and I admire him for doing so', said Ted Reddington, of Ardrossan Court. 'I totally back him, agree with all he says, and congratulate him on his honesty.' His wife, Doris, strongly agreed, and hailed

Mr Mallon as the real voice of the town. 'He's very much in touch with what most people feel', she said.

Ronald Ince, who lives in Seaton Carew, was delighted to read Mr. Mallon's comments in Monday's *Mail*. 'He's only saying what everyone in the town is saying in the pubs and between their friends', said Mr. Ince. 'I for one fully support him and think his bosses should do the same ...'

Nesseel Skirving [a burglary victim] ... is relieved to see a prominent and powerful police officer speak up for people like him. 'Nearly 50 per cent of the town has been affected by crime ... At the moment criminals are laughing at the law. Mr. Mallon is speaking for the people of the town who have to deal with the day-to-day reality of crime.'

Two more victims, Connie Haywood, from Greatham, and Doris Baines, of Blakelock Road, added their names to the hat of unanimous support for the senior detective. Both wholeheartedly agree with him and say he has touched the huge concern most people are feeling about crime and how best to deal with the problem. Dozens of other people in the Middleton Grange Shopping Centre ... gave a spirited thumbs up to Mr. Mallon's comments. 'They are the best and truest words I've read for years', said one.

The chair of the Hartlepool Crime Prevention Panel, who had worked with Victim Support for fourteen years, said that law-abiding families are being let down by the courts.

I defend and support Mr Mallon to the hilt (she said). I have seen society become more and more terrorized by the criminal element and more and more let down by the present government, the judiciary and the magistrates. The meeting on Saturday demonstrated that the people of Hartlepool reflect the mood of people across the country. We have had enough of this soft touch towards those who break the law. ... If we ordinary citizens can see what is happening in society, why on earth can't the government? I can tell you why they can't. It is simply because they do not live in the real world. Ray Mallon is the best thing to happen to Hartlepool since sliced bread.

In answer to a request from the magistrates to specify cases, Mallon gave the following examples:

- A 15-year-old was arrested eighteen times in just fifteen months for offences such as robbery, threatening behaviour, burglary and criminal damage. He was given an 18-month suspension order. In the next six months he was arrested a further ten times for assault, burglary, attempted burglary, criminal damage and shop-lifting. When he was finally taken back to court, the magistrates simply revoked the previous suspension order and replaced it with another one for 18 months.

- A gang attacked a policeman who tried to break up a drunken brawl in Hartlepool. The policeman sustained a double fracture of the cheek-bone, serious cuts to the head, bite marks on a leg and a ripped ear, and lost two teeth. Only three of the assailants were sentenced. The one who received the heaviest punishment was found guilty of wounding with intent. This crime carries a maximum sentence of life imprisonment. But he received a two-year prison sentence, of which he served only twelve months.

- A woman suffered a three-year ordeal of violence at the hands of her husband. The police arrested him 14 times for assault and breach of the peace before he was remanded in custody. He applied for bail and was released by the crown court judge's order. The next day he was again arrested for another incident at his home, and another string of offences followed.

Ray Mallon was publicly backed by the Cleveland police, whose spokesman said that he probably echoed 'the feelings and frustrations of many officers—not only in the county but in the country as a whole'. The commander of the Hartlepool police division, Paul Garvin, announced publicly that he backed Mallon 'all the way'.

In an open letter to the magistrates two of the town's prominent community leaders, a Labour councillor and the chairman of the Owton Fens Community Action Group, called on them to show 'unequivocal support to the police'. It asked them to 'join with the local community in demanding a review of the powers and duties of the magistrates and the role and efficiency of the Crown Prosecution Service, to enable the magistrates to take a stronger position to exact firm punishment on the minority who make life so difficult for the people of Hartlepool'. They also wrote to Peter Mandelson, MP, asking him to 'press the Home Office for a solution to juvenile and "nuisance" crime'.

A Liberal Democrat councillor urged the local newspaper to 'hail his attack on the courts'. It was about time, she said, that someone had 'spoken up for the people'.

Significantly for the much wider influence of this speech and the public reaction to it, 'Mr Mandelson fully backed DCI Mallon's comments and said he thought the vast majority of people in Hartlepool would also support him'. It went without saying that any suspect must be dealt with according to the due processes of the law. For the protection of the innocent justice must be fair; and for the safeguard of the system it must be seen to be fair. But inherently the *guilty* had no 'right' to be found innocent; that right was to defend the innocent, not them. The police and the magistrates, Mr. Mandelson said, were facing 'defiant, smart, experienced criminals of whatever age, many of whom have clever lawyers on hand to take advantage of any chink or weakness in the process'. The MP said that he would not hesitate to question any part of the system that was letting down the side that was fighting crime.[33]

When Lord Chief Justice Taylor said that criminals were not afraid of prison, but were afraid of being caught by the police, Ray Mallon publicly disagreed. He told a meeting of 80 Neighbourhood Watch co-ordinators in Seaton Carew that criminals had no need to fear being caught if they did not fear that they would be punished if they were caught. 'The police do very well in arresting criminals in extremely difficult circumstances with the odds stacked in favour of the accused person ... What deters criminals is the likelihood of them being *caught, convicted and sentenced to imprisonment for periods which fit the crime.* All public services are accountable to the people, but it seems to me that the judiciary is accountable to no-one.'[34]

DCI Mallon addressed many public meetings, both to reinforce his media message, and to gauge what the people who attended the meetings thought about crime, policing, and the general system of law and order. In the month of May 1996, for example, he addressed 2,000 people at 36 public meetings in Hartlepool alone. The attendance at a single meeting was sometimes as high as 300. As knowledge of Hartlepool's new policing spread, he found himself invited to meetings in other towns and counties.[35] His message was that the criminal was now contemptuous of the law-abiding public and of the law-abiding public's reaction to his depredations:

> I want to get rid of the fear of crime so that people can feel safe when they walk down the street and when they are sitting in their own homes—if they can't do that they are not truly free. The criminals have taken over our ground over the years. I want it back ... Our voices are already being heard across the country. People know that families in Hartlepool are fed up with crime.[36]

'Image is important, *but only to show substance.*' The crime strategy involved persuading the public directly, not by 'image-making', but by results, that the police were effective on their behalf.

> I received a letter signed by 20 people about crime and anti-social behaviour. I invited the writer of the letter to a meeting two days later. We showed her the truth about Hartlepool's united front. The chief of the uniformed branch was there. So was the co-ordinator of Neighbourhood Watch.
>
> The organizer of the petition said, 'It is very nice of you to see me, and so soon. I appreciate it. *I know you can't do anything about it*'.
>
> I said, 'Don't say that! We cannot eradicate crime and anti-social behaviour. But we can do something. We are very positive here!'
>
> I took her along to the CID. While she was standing there with me I said, 'What should we do?' The detectives said, 'We should go out there and make it happen!'
>
> That was the Thursday. By the Monday there was no problem, and sixteen suspects had been locked up. In a place as small and settled as Hartlepool, that sort of thing feeds round. There's more confidence in the police. There's more support for the police. Police work is easier. The morale of the law-abiding elements is raised, and the morale of the law-breaking elements is sapped.

This kind of treatment depends, again, on the small scale of the Hartlepool operation, and the possibility, therefore, of the dynamic impulse being applied directly from the top to the ordinary member of the public.

In relation to members of the public, as in the relation of the officers to one another, Mallon insisted on 'gentlemanliness'. When the movement to denigrate men and represent the family as a mechanism through which they could 'legally' abuse their physical superiority in brutally dominating women and children, the detractors had to turn to the French language—male 'chauvinism', and the Italian—'machismo'. There was no English word that suited their purpose. For the English ideal of male conduct was that of the gentleman, and the word 'gentleman' is untranslated in many languages as a description of peculiarly English masculine conduct.

Orwell was able to talk, still in 1941, of the 'extreme gentleness' and 'deeply moral attitude to life' of the Englishman. 'The gentleness of English civilization', he wrote, 'is perhaps its most marked characteristic. You notice it the instant you set foot on

English soil. It is a land where the bus conductors are good tempered and the policemen carry no revolvers ... In the 1914-18 war the songs which the soldiers made up and sang of their own accord were not vengeful but humorous and mock defeatist. The only enemy they ever named was the sergeant-major.'[37]

What is Orwell's reputation (untarnished to this day)? It is that he was one of the most honest and accurate reporters who has ever lived. So it is at least a bold step for anyone fifty years and more later to say that he or she knows more than Orwell about English men at that time.

Once again, Hartlepool is an interesting case, for this strategy aroused little resistance. In London (or, say, Bristol), by contrast, attitudes that would block gentlemanly conduct at work which had been latent and dormant, suddenly became manifest and active, relevant and problematical. Especially after the riots in Brixton and elsewhere in 1981, police in the areas where they had occurred had to face the necessity of a massive re-orientation in their attitude to the public, while in Hartlepool day-by-day policing in practice hardly raised the issue at all.

Obscenities had always been part of working-class culture, but they were essentially situation-specific. One of the main functions of using words tabooed in most contexts was to signify the solidarity of men (and to a lesser extent women) who were sharing the same stressful and difficult situation. With the exception of certain words that were not regarded as 'really swearing' if used in light conversation by a man, like 'bloody' and in the north east of England (surprisingly) 'y'bugger', obscenity and blasphemy had not spilled out into family life and everyday speech. Mallon had no objection to appropriate situation-specific swearing, but discouraged swearing among officers in the presence of members of the public, as counter-productive for police work.

He also discouraged 'unnecessary slovenliness'. A CID officer can be very properly dressed for the job at hand in trainers and jeans, ready for business. But he was not properly dressed if dirty or ragged trainers and jeans were his habitual wear.

Within these apparently trivial and currently devalued details of the *modus operandi* of an effective team, with good long-term relations with as many of the members of the public as possible, the police officer could more effectively use the minimum amount of *controlled* aggression—legally-controlled, custom-controlled, and self-controlled aggression—when it was required.

The Mallon Paradigm

The 'Mallon paradigm' can be summarized along one dimension as outlining his strategy—the 'what?', his tactics—the 'how?', and the four sets of people whose co-operation in pursuing the strategy and tactics had to be secured—the work-force, the management, the media and the public. All elements of this paradigm had to be implemented successfully. 'Take out any one, and you fail.' Of particular importance, then, was the interaction between, and the mutually reinforcing influence of, good management, a well-motivated police force, media support, and public confidence.

Along another dimension the strategy and tactics could be seen as the aims and methods on *paper*, and the motivation of the workforce, management, media and public as the work that brought the strategy and tactics to *life*. In that sense also some phases were more important than others: 'motivation is everything'. Zero-tolerance or confident policing cannot therefore be transferred from one area to another simply as, so to speak, an aspiration, or as a bureaucratic or documentary scheme.

When it was known that he would be leaving the town to take up a more senior post at the Middlesbrough headquarters, regret was widely expressed that the town was losing him. The Labour Mayor of the borough said that he hoped to see him back in Hartlepool, perhaps as a Superintendent; or that he would take charge of the whole of the county force as Chief Constable. Other Labour councillors were also dismayed at losing him. The Labour councillor for Greatham said: 'My only concern is that things carry on in the same vein.'[38]

The town's newspaper summed up his achievements and standing in this report:

> Families in Hartlepool call him 'the best thing since sliced bread'—criminals send him hate mail—but love him or hate him, Ray Mallon is unlikely to be forgotten.
>
> The most successful DCI Hartlepool has had in years, he has spent the last twenty-eight months coming down hard on the criminal element—slashing crime in the town by more than a third.
>
> DCI Mallon has gone out of his way to meet the public to find out what they want from him and his team.

Results have been achieved with the backing of his bosses and the whole of Hartlepool's force—detectives as well as the uniform branch.[39]

His successor, DCI Graham Strange, made it clear that the strategy would be unchanged. 'I have been through it all with Ray in the last two years and I am in total agreement with his policy. We will not give them a chance to gain any ground. We are going to continue exactly in the same way, nothing is going to change.'[40]

Crime and Culture
in Hartlepool

Norman Dennis and Ray Mallon

R AY MALLON regarded all of the work we have discussed so far as 'short-term' strategy. He was interested also in the long-term strategy that would address the roots of crime that the police could not reach. Police work takes place within a community with its own particular characteristics that have developed out of its own particular history. The specific police function is more effectively carried out when there is a good understanding of the 'basic causes', and less effectively when the police's (and the general public's) understanding of the 'basic causes' is flawed.

What kind of place was the Hartlepool within which the crime strategy was implemented? What other 'causes' (a dangerous word) of crime were operating there in the past and in the present? Which of them were under the potential control of the police to limit, which not?

The Upward Surge in Crime 1955-1994

It was almost exactly coincident with the period of what was labelled by later historians 'The Age of Affluence 1951-1964' that crime began to surge upwards.[1] In contrast, during the long period of what R.S. Sayers called 'The Battered Economy 1914-1939', when Hartlepool received a worse battering than most, the crime rate by the standards of the 1990s was extraordinarily low.[2]

While the Plan for Hartlepool of 1948 did not mention crime at all, crime prevention was a major topic of the Plan for Hartlepool of 1994. 'The Borough Council seeks the creation of a physical environment conducive to the overall safety of the community.'

Design and layout had to make it easier to detect 'potential' offenders and more difficult for crimes to be committed.[3]

Crime prevention was also by the 1990s a principal justification in the search for government grants. In the Single Regeneration Budget scheme to improve the two post-war estates, enhanced 'community safety' was one of the six main objectives.[4] In this Hartlepool resembled other British towns. Sunderland, for example, received ('scooped') an additional government grant of £18 million for one of its housing estates, Pennywell, where already 204 government and private agencies were operating. The first use of the money listed was 'tackling crime'.[5]

Hartlepool's Ethnic Homogeneity

The similarities between the crime and policing experiences of New York and Hartlepool are all the more instructive because the two places are otherwise so entirely different.

New York is the vast New World metropolis of divergent ethnic groups. It has been the magnet for all *avant garde* elements in literature, drama and the visual arts that mould public opinion, principally now in their advocacy of libertarianism, moral relativism, and contempt for 'respectability'.

Far from being the natural home of cultural deconstructionism, in the days of the music hall 'Hartlepool' was shorthand for the least promising destination for the person in search of even the hum-drum deviance of anonymous sexual adventure and an exciting night life.

Far from being first the melting pot of diverse nationalities, and then a multi-cultural city—New York's history—Hartlepool is quintessentially an English town, both in its ethnic composition and development.[6] Because Hartlepool's main experience in this century has been of emigration, rather than immigration, the population is predominantly of people born and brought up in the town. Fewer than one per cent of the population at the time of the Census of 1991 were from minority ethnic groups. Of that one per cent, the vast majority were either Chinese or from the Indian sub-continent. Their main contribution to Hartlepool's life can be read from the street facades—'Hot Pot Kebabs', 'Tandoori Night', 'Dilshad Tandoori Indian Restaurant', 'Romantic Palace Chinese Restaurant'. In Hartlepool's problem wards the ethnic minority figures are even lower.[7] None of Hartlepool's problems of crime and sub-criminal disorder stem to any significant extent, therefore, from ethnic diversity, either from the side of the immigrants themselves or from the English population's reaction to immigration.

What we see in Hartlepool with extreme clarity, therefore, is the emergence of high rates of crime in *English* culture alone, among *English* boys and young men, with little 'contamination' in scientific terms from complicating factors within the town itself.

Until international youth culture began to split the generations in the late 1950s, Hartlepool was a homogeneous town with a continuous history from Anglo-Saxon times. It survived the rapine of the Danes in 800, withstood the wrath of Robert the Bruce when Edward II chose the port for his return from Bannockburn, and was occupied by the Scots during the English Civil War. The town is still famous even outside its borders for an incident of overzealous patriotism during the Napoleonic Wars. In 1914 it was shelled by the German fleet at the cost of 128 lives in Hartlepool and West Hartlepool, with a further 400 wounded. In return fire Hartlepool's own guns inflicted significant damage on the German battle cruisers.[8] Later in the war it was bombed from the air by zeppelins. In 1919 the town was awarded a battle tank as a trophy because it had contributed more per head to the War Funds than any other town.[9] In the Second World War it was bombed by the Luftwaffe in 43 air raids with the loss of 70 civilian lives.[10] When Victoria Road was redeveloped in the 1970s, the name Victoria remained, and the war memorial was embellished, not demolished.

Inscribed on the memorial are the names of more than 1,500 local men 'who at their country's call left all that was dear to them to hazard their lives that others might live in freedom'. 'Living in freedom' meant, not the freedom to be a bully, a thief or an idler at other people's expense. It meant the freedom secured to decent people by adherence to the concrete operating rules, standards and manners of national and borough government, of an unarmed police force, of an independent judiciary, of the Royal and Ancient Order of Duffaloes, of neighbourliness, of playing for West Hartlepool Rugby Union Club, of supporting Sunderland AFC, of the Wesleyan Chapel, of Christ Church, of being a teacher, of being a pupil, of being a grandfather, of being a pit deputy, an able seaman, a dock worker, a fisherman or a bus driver, of roast beef and Yorkshire pudding as a normally achievable Sunday dinner in one way or another—of the 'British way of life' as actually lived and experienced in Hartlepool. When a former Labour long-serving MP for Hartlepool died at the end of 1996, among the tributes paid to him on the local radio was that he had been 'a patriot' as well as 'a gentleman'.[11]

Hartlepool's Small Size and Geographical Compactness

Far from being a city coping with enormous population growth in the twentieth century, like New York, the present borough's size of 90,000 is not much changed from the population of its predecessor towns and villages at the time of the First World War. It is the kind of community that contains a large proportion of people with shared memories.[12]

Hartlepool is geographically compact. The built-up area stretches only about two miles to the north of the town centre, two miles to the south and two miles to the west.

Material Hardship and Low Crime Rates Before the 1960s

Hartlepool's period of growth was the second half of the nineteenth century and the first two decades of the twentieth. It grew rapidly in the 1830s and 1840s after Stephenson's new steam locomotive, the Locomotion, had proved its worth on the world's first public railway line which ran from Hartlepool's neighbouring town of Stockton to Darlington. Lines were rapidly constructed from the pits of south-west Durham to carry its coal to a new dock. The streets of the nineteenth-century industrial town were named after the east coast English ports familiar to the seamen on the collier brigs, and their havens from the North Sea's fatal storms—Scarborough, Kings Lynn, Whitby. Other docks were opened in 1847-54 and West Hartlepool was founded in the fields to the south of old Hartlepool to service them. By 1890 Hartlepool was the third busiest port in England, after London and Liverpool. With the development of the large collieries of the concealed coalfield in south-east Durham after 1900, Hartlepool's importance as a port exporting coal and importing pit props was further enhanced. Ship-owning became an important element in Hartlepool's economy.[13]

It grew most rapidly after the 1850s when the discovery of iron ore only 15 miles away in the Cleveland Hills—so close to rich coal and limestone reserves—turned Teesside overnight into the world's greatest centre of iron, and later steel, production. From being mainly a coal and timber port, Hartlepool became an important centre not only of iron and steel production, but also of ship-building and marine engineering.[14]

1913 was the town's most prosperous year, when it produced more ships and more iron and steel, caught more fish, exported more coal and imported more timber than before or since.

The rise in working-class crime in Hartlepool after the 1950s can by no means be attributed to the sudden emergence of unusual, or unusually severe, *economic* problems, or to a sudden deterioration in housing or other factors in the *physical* environment after the 1950s.

Relying as it did on the few basic industries of shipping, shipbuilding, iron and steel production, fishing and coal Hartlepool had shared the long dismal inter-war fate of the other North Sea towns of Durham. The loss of ships due to enemy action in the First World War, the wartime lack of maintenance of the mercantile fleet and then the slump that followed the brief post-war boom crippled Hartlepool's ship-owners and brought hardship to the merchant seamen. By 1939 there were only eight local ship-owners left. During the depression of the early 1930s the yards in Hartlepool were almost totally inactive. Some yards were permanently closed by National Shipbuilders Security Ltd., whose 'rationalization' schemes are better known in relation to Jarrow on the Tyne, 'the town that was murdered'.[15] All Hartlepool's shipyards except Gray's were put out of business.

In the year 1936-37 nearly one in ten of all insured males in Hartlepool left for the Midlands and Home Counties (with others going elsewhere) under a government scheme of assistance to workers migrating to the more prosperous regions of the country.[16]

Gray's shipyard was still optimistic enough in the 1920s to build a garden village in the town, Graythorp, to house its workers at the Greatham Creek yard, and the demand for ships during the Second World War restored activity to the yard. But after the war international competition forced Gray's, too, into liquidation.[17] Post-war modernization of the British Steel plants raised great if consciously fragile hopes. But steel production, too, was eventually lost, being relocated to Redcar.

In the nineteenth century Hartlepool either retained or improved the *cultural* conditions of working-class life that suppressed crime and quality-of-life offences as a way of handling problems, whether those problems were economic, domestic, educational, or arose in any other sector of life.

In the years of Hartlepool's Victorian and Edwardian prosperity, as well as its roads, railways, water mains and sewerage system, docks, coal staithes, blast furnaces, lime works, shipyards and factories, imposing churches, chapels, government buildings, and libraries had been constructed; parks had been laid out; the suffrage had been extended to all working men and democratic local government had been established; and the great working-class institutions of collective self-help were founded and developed—chapels, trade unions, football clubs, retail co-operatives, friendly societies.

The home of the West Hartlepool Literary and Mechanics Institute, the Athenaeum Building, completed in 1851, and Christ Church, completed in 1854, were constructed out of limestone excavated from the docks. The massive Wesley Church in Victoria Road was built in 1872, with an imposing stone facade, including a Corinthian portico. The red brick and terra cotta Public Library was built in 1894. The Empire Theatre, later the cinema, was opened in 1909. The architectural symbol of working-class achievement was the Co-operative Stores of 1913, built of Portland stone, with a 100 feet high neo-classical cupola. It is still one of the town's most impressive buildings.

Ward Jackson Park was opened in 1883. In the 1880s Jackson still was honoured as the founding father of the town. He had fallen on hard times, and money was collected to provide him with an annuity, but he died before the gift could be made. The money was therefore used to create for the general public a typical Victorian park, with a lake and formal and informal gardens. In Edwardian times it was embellished with an elaborate fountain and bandstand. The Victorian and Edwardian industrial and commercial élite built their mansions in spacious, well-wooded grounds around it, with a complete lack of any sense, or any premonition, that a public park in the neighbourhood could ever become a drawback, as the scene of wanton destruction, defacement, and personal danger. The fountain and bandstand were restored in the 1990s.

In terms of control over their own affairs, from 1847 to 1865 the residents of West Hartlepool lived in a classic 'company town', benefiting from the 'fearless speculation' but under the 'almost dictatorial powers' of Ward Jackson, the promoter of the Harbour and Dock Company.[18] The charter of incorporation was acquired by West Hartlepool in 1887, giving it its own town council, with the local ship-building magnate Sir William Gray as the first mayor. West Hartlepool was a county borough from 1902 to 1974. With fair and free elections, but with little working-class representation, it wielded increasingly wide powers granted under central government legislation and under central government control over education, cleansing, public works, and, under the local Watch Committee, the police.

Criminal and unruly elements in the town were restrained by the new police, modelled on Sir Robert Peel's Metropolitan Police of 1829. The style of policing by the 'bobbies' was symbolized in Hartlepool by the architecture of their headquarters. When the old Police Station was built in the 1870s, it was not in the style of a threatening barracks, but of a late-Georgian house. The British policeman, whose own unarmed confidence was based on the confidence that the law-abiding population put in him, and he in them, was the astonishment and admiration of the world until far into the twentieth century.[19]

We have already said that the rise in working-class crime in the second half of the twentieth century cannot be attributed to a deterioration in economic and material conditions. Nor can the low crime rates of the Victorian and Edwardian period and later be attributed to the *economic* prosperity and salubrious *material* environment of the working-class population then as compared with the 1990s.

Even when West Hartlepool was prosperous for the bourgeoisie, life was not easy or predictable for working people. The westerly winds blew pollution away from the big houses around Ward Jackson Park. The workers in the town had to breath it in. Before new coal staithes were built in 1909, coal dust sometimes lay ankle deep in the residential streets of Middleton, and crunched underfoot as one walked around the district until coal exports ceased. The North Works of the steel company were near the centre of the town, the South Works not far to the south of it. Nearly all the jobs were arduous and dangerous, especially for the men who went to sea, and very few of them were secure. Before the de-casualization scheme after the Second World War, dock labour was notoriously irregular. The demand for iron and steel, depending as it did upon capital expenditure elsewhere in the economy, was deeply affected by the trade cycle. So was the demand for new ships, which made shipbuilding a wildly fluctuating activity. In the 1880s, for example, the highest annual tonnage built in Britain was three times the lowest, and between 1900 and 1913 the best was twice the worst. The industry therefore attracted special attention from economists when they analyzed unemployment and the causes of poverty.[20]

Work in the shipyards was not only severely subject to the trade cycle, it was 'lumpy' in that men were paid off between the time that one ship was launched and the keel of the next was laid.

All the anguish of unemployment today—boredom, a feeling of uselessness, a low income, humiliation—applied then. But added to all that, as compared to today's unemployed, the income of the unemployed in the nineteenth century and until well into the twentieth century was much lower and their material conditions were far inferior.

At the beginning of its life West Hartlepool was 'fortunate in being established late in the industrial revolution, avoiding the worst aspects of squalor noticeable in the earliest industrialization of old Hartlepool'.[21] But a century later its working-class housing stock was in every respect poor. According to the 1948 planning survey of West Hartlepool, out of Hartlepool's 19,000 dwellings, over 2,700 were 'badly blighted', with no baths, shared w.c.s, and crowded at more than 50 to the acre. An additional 5,300 were sub-standard.[22] The 1951 Census shows that more than nine per cent of Hartlepool's households lived at more than 1.5 persons per room.

In 1951 nearly half of all Hartlepool's households (49 per cent) lacked one or more of the five 'basic household amenities' recorded by the Census, and 13 per cent were without any piped water in their dwelling. The 1951 Census did not record whether the water closet was outside the dwelling—by far the commonest arrangement in working-class districts. Only in a later Census did an internal water closet and tapped hot water become basic amenities the lack of which was to be recorded.

The infant mortality rate in 1955-57 was 43 per 1000 live births—the worst rate of the 157 large towns of England and Wales. Tuberculosis was still an anxiety in working-class families; in 1957 98 new cases were notified in Hartlepool. Hartlepool's death rate from bronchitis was the twelfth worst.

In 1951 more than 68 per cent of the population of Hartlepool had left school before their fifteenth birthday.

But through all these difficulties, the culture of the family remained intact. It is estimated, indeed, that between a third to a half of assisted migrants could not settle away from home, and returned to their families.

Crime was not considered a possible solution to one's personal frustration, at any age, by any but a tiny minority of the population. When the population of England and Wales was 20 million in 1861, 88,500 crimes were recorded. In 1901, when the population had *risen by 60 per cent*, and when more and more police forces were being established (i.e the likelihood of a crime being recorded was being increased), the number of recorded crimes had actually *fallen by over eight per cent*. Hartlepool's share in these figures meant that by present-day standards its crime rate must have been exceedingly low. Recorded crimes grew only slowly up to 1955.[23] In spite of the fact that the study of the town in 1947 by the Max Lock group was partly carried out by the famous sociologist Ruth Glass, the report does not mention crime, vandalism or law and order as issues in Hartlepool at all.[24]

Material Improvements and Rising Crime Since the 1960s

Since the beginning of the 1960s the story is one of improvement in education, housing, working-class representation, and the economy—and of course of vast improvements in all these respects on the 1920s and 1930s.[25]

There is still 'heavy' industry, now lightened by the use of machinery for lifting and conveying. The pungent smell of the mangesite works still penetrates into the houses around the rugby football ground. The nuclear power station casts its shadow onto the mud flats of the Tees. The chemical factories string south towards Billingham. Public and private investment has improved the fish quay and made the 400 jobs that depend on it more secure. The Tees and Hartlepool Port Authority has added a deep water berth at Victoria Dock and the north harbour is again busy and profitable. As in the days when the storage yards presented an astonishing spectacle of hundreds of thousands of pit props, timber is again the port's staple; three-quarters of its trade is in forestry products.

But the reliance on declining heavy industries that had been such a burden to the town ever since the First World War was being reduced in ways and to an extent unimagined in the 1930s. Public policy was now to bring work to Hartlepool, and not to pressure young people to leave home to find work elsewhere. The Korean electronics giant, Samsung, located a £600 million factory in the borough. Other Asian firms have come as suppliers to Samsung. Small firms begin to make in aggregate an impact upon the local economy. The town is now the European centre for a Hong Kong producer of mountain bikes. Public money has been used to help local firms like Specialist Welding and Fabrication to develop and diversify. Since 1987 the Teesside Development Corporation has been responsible for Union Dock and Jackson Dock, and has created construction jobs in the first place, intending to create tourist jobs in the long run, based on the free-spending owners of the luxury yachts in the marina, and the visitors to the new quayside museum, restored men o' war, and other attractions.

In 1970 High-Street shopping was relocated to the purpose-built Middleton Grange Centre. In the mid-1990s £6 million of private investment was spent on roofing it over and on other improvements.[26] The circulation spaces of Middleton Grange are somewhat less luxurious in their ambience than the nationally-known Gateshead Metrocentre, or the Bridges in the much larger town of Sunderland. But—whether you like them or dislike them—there is very little difference in the decor and the range of goods on sale whether you are in the Metrocentre or in the Middleton Grange Body Shop, MacDonalds, Boots, Woolworths, Marks and Spencer, Dixons, W.H. Smith, or any other of the full range of High-Street shops Middleton Grange possesses. Although the Grainger Market in Newcastle is certainly a more salubrious building, the stalls there are not so very different in what they offer from the stalls in Hartlepool.

The opportunities for education have been transformed since the 1950s. Obviously, no one leaves school now while they are not yet 15 years of age except as a permanent truant. Opposite the old Police Station is the large modern College of Art and Design. In 1993 Hartlepool entered a competition arranged by the government scheme called 'City Challenge'. The town won £37 million of public money, to be allocated over a five-year period. The College of Further Education, two major extensions of which were funded by City Challenge, now takes up much of the eastern side of Stockton Street.

In Hartlepool in 1991 19 per cent of males and 20 per cent of females aged 16-24 were students.[27] Again, these facilities and opportunities for the sons and daughters of working people, and for working people themselves when they are retired, were only dreamed of in Hartlepool forty years before.[28] A large and well-equipped library was opened five years ago, with facilities of access, technology, and assistance from trained and helpful staff not inferior for most practical purposes to a university library.

From being a company town, in terms of political representation, Hartlepool is now governed by a council elected on the suffrage of all men and women aged 18 and older. It is firmly in the hands of the working-class party. By 1996 there were 39 Labour councillors against only three Conservatives (one of whom was an Independent Conservative). There were seven Liberal Democrats. As we have already remarked, the local MP, Peter Mandelson, is widely credited with exerting great influence on the creation of the political doctrine and the electoral strategy of the 1990s' Labour Party. The adjacent constituency, Sedgefield, is represented in Parliament by Tony Blair, the leader of the Labour Party nationally, and therefore the United Kingdom's prime-minister-in-waiting. No reasonable case can be made that the rise in crime has been due to increasing—the term that is used so much—'exclusion'.

Unemployment and insecurity of employment have been major features of working-class life in the Hartlepools during its whole existence as an industrial town (with the exception of the brief experience in the 1950s and 1960s, when unemployment dropped, though not to levels the south of England at that time regarded as 'full employment'). At times both in the nineteenth century and during the interwar period fewer than 60 per cent of the men had been in employment. Unemployment returned as a stubborn problem in the 1970s, though at no time did it approach the worst rates of the 1930s. In 1996 only 82 per cent of

Hartlepool's economically-active males were employed, and 94 per cent of the economically-active females.[29]

One reaction to the increased freedom made possible by the higher standard of housing, education, income in employment—and social security when not in employment—has been the decline of working-class self-improvement, not only educationally and politically, but morally.

The working men's clubs were once schools of a wide and humane sociability, of self-improvement, and unapologetically of 'virtuous conduct', making an important contribution to what John Stuart Mill called 'the cultivation of the political intelligence of the nation'.[30] The membership card of a working men's club even in the 1980s showed pictures of late Victorian or Edwardian men and youths attending a lecture, studying in a library, painting at an easel and so forth. On the card are the exhortations: 'Honour all men; love the brother; use hospitality to one another; be not forgetful to entertain strangers'. The clubs' activities are decoratively displayed on the card: visits to public works and parks, natural history, botany, music, recitations, debates, essays, lending libraries, lectures, readings, friendly societies, trade societies and penny banks. 'Taste' and 'self-restraint' are listed. An angel shelters under her right wing a representation of 'Recreation', with cricket bat, rugby and soccer ball, and billiard cue. Under her left wing 'Study' works before a globe at his desk.[31]

The working men's clubs were one of the most important places where everyday usage gave the working man experience of the benefits of *rule-bound* democracy. To a diminished extent they still are. Each member holds a copy of the conditions under which his own club may control his conduct within the rules, and expel him within the rules of specification of the charge, notice of summons, the right to defend himself and the right of appeal against the committee's decision on his case. They were the working-class academies of how decency and fair play could be realized within the context of a consensual social order.

His club's committee was the working man's constant reminder that his freedom to enjoy his drink in peace, and go about his reasonable business without being interfered with, depended upon a complex system of agreed manners backed ultimately by sanctions, and was not something that emerged automatically when everyone did as he liked. The chairman was there to ensure that only precise business was attended to—the seconded motion and the seconded amendments before the meeting—and that all sides had their say, without aggression or filibustering. The secretary was there to produce a conclusive record of decisions—the subsequent unchallengability of the record depending on the committee's subsequent approval of it as the correct one. Devices such as the vote of no confidence in the chairman were a defence against the abuse of his office. The annual general meeting was the occasion on which officers who were not doing their job honestly or efficiently could be replaced by a majority of the ordinary members present and voting.[32]

Nothing could be further in spirit from the culture of the Rave. The Athenaeum is today the location of a homely 'caff'. The Buffs Social Club in Church Street is the remnant of the great friendly society movement that once thrived in the town. Renamed The Venue, the old building of the Co-operative Retail Society has been converted with government funding to provide Hartlepool today with 'new entertainment facilities', namely, a night club. Government funds channelled through City Challenge were used to remake the old Town Hall, too, into an 'entertainments venue'.[33]

The old culture and 'public education' which had invited 'the Englishman from his youth' to use his liberty and to associate for mutual self-improvement, to 'fear nothing, to be astonished at nothing, and to save himself by his own exertions from every sore strait in life',[34] was gradually, though by no means fully, replaced by one which invited the youth to see all his troubles as being outside of his own responsibility and control; as someone else's fault; and for someone else to remedy ... or else.

A second reaction to material improvements has been the decline in religion. In 1996-97, after lying abandoned and derelict for many years, the Wesleyan Church in the town centre was being restored with government funds to provide the town with yet another night-club, a sauna, and shops. The Church of England's Christ Church was deconsecrated and closed in 1974. £2 million of the City Challenge money was spent in making the building into a tourist information centre and art gallery.

A third reaction to what, in comparison with the period from 1913 to the end of the Second World War, has been a period of peace and material improvement (with unemployment marring the picture but not on an inter-war scale), has been the destruction of the family. It remains, of course, the personal choice of a large majority of the population as a 'life-style', with at least the initial shared ambition to maintain their own marriage as a more-or-less permanent arrangement. But *as a strictly defined and defended social institution*, largely indifferent to the convenience of their own marriage and their own married parenthood for spouses who found they did not get on with one another, it has been severely and probably irreparably weakened since the 1960s. Writing about the family, Jonathan Sacks distinguishes between what he calls the 'politics of institutions' and the 'politics of interest'.[35] The existence of benign institutions depends upon a lively sense of the common good. Their dismemberment can be quite cheerfully accomplished by influential individuals or special-interest pressure groups and their supporters, either out of misplaced good intentions or resentment against their personal hardships.

As late as 1957 nearly 96 per cent of all Hartlepool children were still being born to married parents.[36] By 1991 the proportion of children born outside of marriage in Hartlepool had increased ten-fold. Not four per cent, but 43 per cent of children were—to use the 1957 term—illegitimate.[37] The family had also weakened among the well-to-do, who had been foremost in promoting and celebrating its abandonment. Their financial and other strengths allowed them to adopt a régime of sexual freedom without the detriments to their children and their neighbours rapidly making themselves obvious. But when they did appear, then they pulled back towards the family. From being more libertarian than the poor in the 1957 they were now far more family-oriented than the poor.[38]

The fourth reaction to the problems of finding employment, one of the last remaining from the myriad problems of the previous 150 years, was closely related to family breakdown. That reaction was to indulge in growing youth crime, drug abuse and sub-criminal disorder. For now, whether he himself had been brought up in a lone-parent family or by both his own parents, the boy no longer had the same pressures upon him as in the past to see his own life in the perspective of monogamous marriage and intimate and continuous parental responsibility during the long years of dependency of his own children. The removal of controls over pre-marital sex, and of 'scandal' from lone motherhood, cohabitation, abortion and divorce had altered all that. He could respond much more self-centredly to his own frustrations. The boy who was himself brought up in a single-parent, cohabiting or re-constituted family, already had a far slacker, less committed and indefinite circle of kin, whose good opinion of his conduct he might value—or who indeed themselves might have any special reason to care about what he did.

The poor, who had de-institutionalized their kinship structures under the impulse of middle- and upper-class inspired fashions, were left to deal with all the detriments. They had always lacked the financial resources to neutralize them, and they now lacked the cultural resources to reverse the changes that were multiplying the crimes and quality-of-life offences that were increasingly affecting their daily lives. They continued to be bombarded with anti-family propaganda that the middle and upper classes no longer believed. Clare Rayner, one of the most influential Agony Aunts of the period, actually declared as late as January 1997 that sexual probity was 'a luxury'. If you were poor, according to her, you could not *afford* it.[39]

In practical terms this was the opposite of the truth. If the rich could afford a régime of sexual licence, the poor could not. It was also in historical terms complete nonsense. For when working and unemployed people were much poorer, the sexual probity of most of them was, by the standards of their altogether more affluent successors, much higher, and the crime rate, accordingly, much lower.

CONCLUSION

Hartlepool is exceptionally interesting from the point of view of the context within which a police force has to work. It provides a clear example of the volume and origin of crime which is broadly outside the control of the specialized function of the police. For a study of the town shows that while much of the current rhetoric about being 'tough on the causes of crime' assumes that material and external factors such as poverty, unemployment, immigration, 'the inner city', deteriorating education opportunities, poor housing, political exclusion, and so forth constitute those causes, they are very weak in explaining the *rise in crime* in Hartlepool over the past forty years. Hartlepool's history enables us to see clearly that, there at least, it was the decay of the cultural institutions that had excluded crime and quality-of-life offences from the repertoire of responses boys and young men could make to their difficulties, and not a deterioration in their standard of living, that was coincident with the remarkable rise in crime rates it experienced within the span of two generations.

When we turn narrowly to the policing function, a central issue is seen to be that of police and public morale. The 'forbearing use of power' was the ideal of British rule from—at the latest—early in the nineteenth century, in both domestic policing and in imperial administration.[40] 'Zero tolerance' therefore jars on the ears of those who realise that the British style of rule was historically a highly successful use of authority, no less than on the anarchist ears of those who are opposed to the exercise of any authority at all. Zero tolerance originated as a sound-bite in the American media. It is now the firmly established term in Britain also. All we can do as we use it is to point out its pitfalls, and insist that what we mean by the term is the strategy detailed in these two chapters on Hartlepool.

Power was used forbearingly only for so long as it could be exercised confidently. The forbearing use of authority depended upon the existence of a virtuous circle of confident rule, social peace, and therefore support for those in authority. As late as 1955, when there was a great vogue in books studying 'national character', the anthropologist Geoffrey Gorer actually explained the legendary law-abidingness of English working men in terms of their identification with the decent English bobby as their principal role model.[41]

But from the early 1960s this virtuous circle was broken. Crime rose. Explanations for criminal conduct began to predominate that emphasized the importance of massive material and external causes. At the same time it was denied that the frequency of crimes and quality-of-life offences was increasing. The public's view was disparaged as 'populist' and dismissed as 'moral panic'. There was a withdrawal of élite support for policing. (In 1984 the then Bishop of Durham scolded a correspondent with the message that 'cuts are constantly made on those services that are of particular value to the poor, but money can always be found for ... keeping up the police forces. I do not say that we can do without ... police expenditure, but the emphasis does seem to be persistently on non-caring and aggressive directions.')[42] Police morale suffered, and therefore police performance. The confidence of the general public in the police was sapped, and therefore co-operation with the police was reduced. The confidence of the criminal rose.

Crime rose; that crime was rising was denied; but what crime there was, was due to massive material and external forces ...

Not the least part of the success of confident-policing policy in Hartlepool 1994-96 and later lay in the willingness to put the police point of view publicly. The empirical and ethical 'definition of the situation' of crime and quality-of-life offences in the town was not left to the same extent as previously to anti-police pressure groups; carriers of the post-1960s ideology of social work in the probation service and elsewhere; and experts from the universities and the legal profession also produced by the student movements and the more general cultural changes of the 1960s and later.

Hartlepool's experience suggests strongly, therefore, that policing on the Mallon model can effectively cut the crime rate and the volume of quality-of-life offences by at least 20 per cent. But it suggests just as strongly that there has been a deep cultural change, *not least in the conception of what causes crime and how the criminal can be effectively dealt with*, which has shifted the propensity of boys and young men to deal with their difficulties at the expense of the fellow-citizens, rather than in more constructive (or non-destructive) ways. The new culture is one in which boys and young men are no longer being socialized into the major life-project of looking after their own children in their own home, and one in which they are regarded as helpless, or even somehow justified, in succumbing to the 'causes' of their crime—'poverty' and unemployment—through engaging in criminal and anti-social conduct. It can therefore be expected that, for so long as the culture persists, criminal and anti-social conduct will continue at a much higher level than in the past, but with new police strategies bringing the rate of increase under more effective control.

Strathclyde's Spotlight Initiative

John Orr

THE STRATHCLYDE Police Spotlight Initiative was launched on 1 October 1996, its objective being to dramatically reduce violent crime, disorder, and the fear of crime throughout the force area. At the time of writing we are only four months into a long-term strategy which can make a lasting difference.

Before going on to set out what the Spotlight Initiative is, it may be useful to tackle the myths and misconceptions which have surrounded it. Commentators have been keen to sensationalise through comparison with foreign forces and the application of labels such as 'Zero Tolerance'.

Zero Tolerance

One of the misconceptions is that the Spotlight Initiative is a policy of 'Zero Tolerance'. A fast track route to police cells for those caught committing so called minor crimes is neither the intention nor the practice of the Spotlight Initiative.

A fundamental principle of Strathclyde Police is to encourage the use of officer discretion when dealing with offenders. A policy of 'Zero Tolerance', issued from the top, would not only undermine this discretion, but also the compassion and resourcefulness of the individual officer on the street. The public expect the police to use that discretion sensitively and see it as reasonable that, for example, an offender who has dropped litter is given the opportunity to pick it up; that children found drinking alcohol are taken home to their parents; that great thought is given when dealing with any vulnerable person.

Spotlight also deals with issues such as street robberies and offensive weapons where use of the term 'Zero Tolerance' can be tempting. A concern, however, that Strathclyde Police has in using the term, even in such an extreme context, is that it may

104

detract from its current association with domestic violence, a context in which it is rightly and powerfully being applied in Scotland. It is regrettable, but understandable, that the slogan is so readily applied to everything from food hygiene to all crimes.

The aim of the Spotlight Initiative is simply to make the Strathclyde Police area a safer place to live, work, visit and invest. A crackdown on crime it is. Targeting criminals it is. Positive Action against quality-of-life crimes it is. Community policing with the gloves off it is. 'Zero Tolerance' it is not.

Not the Big Apple

It is also worth stating that Strathclyde is *not* New York City. The areas have different environments, cultures and legal systems and the NYPD deal with much higher crime levels. For example, in the past five years Strathclyde Police has recorded an average of 78 homicides annually among a population of 2.25 million people, while New York with a population of 7.25 million experienced an average of 1,418. New York also has a bigger drugs problem, including crack cocaine, ethnic challenges and substantial gun and gang cultures, often featuring juveniles. The two places are very different, and the remedies reflect that.

Strathclyde Police ... a History

A look at the force history, its development and its problems, highlights why the time is now right for Strathclyde Police to introduce a new, invigorated style of policing.

Strathclyde Police originated in 1975, the product of local government re-organisation which included the amalgamation of six police forces in the West Central belt of Scotland. Covering an area of some 5,348 square miles with a current strength of 7,264 police officers and 1,920 support staff, it is by far the largest of the Scottish forces and second or third in Great Britain. The force serves about half the population of Scotland, some two and a quarter million people, and provides a home for three-quarters of all Scottish criminals.

From 1975 it geographically matched and was principally accountable to the newly formed Strathclyde Regional Council. Competing financial demands on the council, notably social services and education, meant that the force was required to operate some 194 officers under its authorised establishment, then 6,954.

A major priority for this new police force was to ensure the integration of the officers, divisions and policies of its composite forces to provide a standard service to the public.

Large, sparsely populated, sometimes affluent, rural areas were now united in the same Region and policed by the same force as heavily populated towns; sprawling suburban conurbations built to accommodate the Glasgow population overspill; and of course, the City of Glasgow itself with its vibrant centre and professional peripheral communities contrasting greatly with its areas of multiple deprivation. The latter were largely responsible for generating a global reputation for the 'Glesga' Hard Man', 'vicious razor gangs', sectarian rivalry, and tenement slums, all of which combined to earn the much publicised label of 'No Mean City'.

It is important to take a more in-depth look at Glasgow, as its influence could not fail to impact on its hinterland. The adage that 'when America sneezes, Britain catches cold' translated to Strathclyde as Glasgow's problems often seemed to second guess those of its surrounding populations, albeit to a lesser extent.

During the 1980s and continuing into the 1990s, considerable investment which targeted community improvement projects in deprived areas such as Drumchapel, Castlemilk, Gorbals, Govan and Easterhouse among others, has formed part of a major regeneration of the city, and Strathclyde as a whole. Run-down housing estates and high-rise tower blocks have been redeveloped or razed to the ground with generally better housing being developed. Of equal significance is the considerable movement of population out of Glasgow to the rest of Strathclyde. Across Strathclyde new employment opportunities and business enterprise zones have been created to replace lost indigenous industries. Community groups have been supported in their efforts to rebuild areas. Strathclyde as a whole, but Glasgow in particular, has undergone a renaissance.

However, despite this radical transformation, the City of Glasgow—now deservedly earning various cultural accolades such as 'City of Culture' and 'City of Architecture'—has found its negative image, perhaps historically deserved, hard to cast off. The 'No Mean City' image remains beloved of the media. Violence made more interesting copy than the reborn Glasgow, with tourists still opting for the squalor depicted by the classic Oscar Marzaroli picture postcards featuring bedraggled street urchins, unshod and unwashed, as their memory of Glasgow. This outmoded image of the City has served to ensure that incidents of crime here attract disproportionate levels of media interest, which consequently engenders an increased and distorted perception of the level of crime, heightening the public's fear of crime. As the lead city of the region, this misleading image also tarnished Strathclyde.

In fairness, throughout the 1970s and 1980s reported crime in Glasgow *did* rise each year. The same was true of Strathclyde and the country as a whole, fuelled by the pernicious onslaught of the drug phenomenon that had already swept across America a decade earlier.

From 1983 the incidence of drugs misuse in Strathclyde increased dramatically. Where only five years before a suspect found in possession of a syringe containing traces of heroin would have been regarded as 'a good capture' for any street officer, such cases now flooded the police forensic laboratory.

Initially, the use of so-called 'hard' drugs was largely confined to the run down peripheral housing estates surrounding Glasgow. Its effect on crime, however, was not so localised. As the 1990s arrived, an estimated 10,000 intravenous heroin users lived in Glasgow. Their preference to inject rather than smoke heroin, a comparatively cheap drug, was unique and over the next decade was to cut short the lives of hundreds of young people. Mixed with other drugs, in particular the gelatinous form of temazepam, 'jellies', it produced a lethal cocktail. Some addicts contracted HIV or Hepatitis from shared needles whilst other users developed ulcers and abscesses which resulted in the amputation of limbs, infection and collapsed or congested veins. For the majority, it resulted in stupefaction; a numb generation, unemployed and unemployable, reliant on state benefits for sustenance, and on the proceeds of crime to buy their next fix. A 'tenner bag' (£10) soon became a 'score bag' (£20) when the victim was well and truly hooked.

Glasgow was seen as the drugs capital of Strathclyde but, as surely as American trends cross the Atlantic to London and radiate further north, the problem could not be contained by the invisible Glasgow boundary. The idyllic rural settings of the most widespread towns and villages across the force were also affected. The despair caused by drug addiction, and the rise in property crime that fed its voracious appetite, became increasingly evident. Housebreaking, car theft, fraud, robbery, disorder and violent crime all rose steeply.

Behind the scenes, the 'Mr Bigs' of drugs, who retained a cool detachment from their despicable stock in trade, were engaged in a violent and bloody battle over territory. The early 1990s heralded the first signs of 'organised crime' or 'gang warfare', as the tabloids dubbed it, since the gangs of the early 1970s. Several shootings and murders amongst the drugs fraternity occurred, but the banner headlines in newspapers did not always reflect the distinction. Ordinary members of the public felt threatened by the violence, although the likelihood of being caught in the crossfire was at worst remote.

Ironically, the preference of the Strathclyde addict for the cheaper drugs such as heroin, amphetamine, cannabis and temazepam, perhaps staved off an even worse fate. The expensive and more sinister cocaine, in particular 'crack', did not succeed in gaining a foothold in Scotland.

By 1991 crime was at its highest level since the inception of Strathclyde Police, and whilst media attention was primarily on Glasgow, with Paisley a secondary focus, a rise in crime was witnessed across the entire force. For the first time, crime involving firearms, particularly armed robberies, became prevalent. Although this was in keeping with the pattern emerging elsewhere across Britain, it was the 'No Mean City' which garnered the majority of public attention.

Something had to be done—and quickly.

The Early 1990s—the Era of the Operation

1990 saw the appointment of Chief Constable Mr Leslie Sharp, my predecessor. In robust fashion, he made successful representation to the local authority seeking funding to recruit up to the authorised level and pledged that Strathclyde Police would deal firmly with serious criminals.

A series of high profile, 90 day Operations were launched to tackle major crime, with the media as active partners. Operation Blade targeted criminals carrying knives, a trend which was so widespread it had almost become accepted as a part of the culture of the West of Scotland; Operation Spur recovered hundreds of criminally held firearms; Operation Interlock reassured the public, encouraging them to have the confidence to give police information following a number of drug-related shootings in Glasgow's East End; Operation Turnkey slashed housebreaking figures; and Operation Eagle tackled drugs dealers, increasing seizures of drugs, reducing supplies and inflating the price of drugs in accordance with the laws of supply and demand.

Such positive policing measures clearly won the support of the public and, from 1992, the previous year-on-year rise in crime was reversed.

A New Chief Constable

On 1 January 1996, when I took over the reins as Chief Constable of Strathclyde, crime had fallen over the previous four years by almost 20 per cent. From Sir Leslie Sharp I inherited a well resourced force with good morale which enjoyed considerable public and local authority support. Serious criminals living and operating in our area knew that the police could and would crack down heavily on their nefarious activities whenever necessary. Several serious crime issues had been successfully tackled by the series of 'operations'.

Despite this success, an independent survey carried out in 1995 showed that fear of crime was rising, with 84 per cent of the public wrongly believing that crime was increasing. A further survey, The Scottish Crime Survey, published in 1996, identified that 92 per cent of the public were concerned about crime and 52 per cent were 'worried that they or someone they lived with would be the victim of crime'. In spite of positive police action, violent crime and disorder were also on the increase and proving difficult to combat. Given that the force had been so successful in tackling all the issues it had set out to tackle, the question had to be asked—why was fear of crime continuing to rise?

The answer, I believe, stemmed from the fact that whilst the force focused its resources on tackling these most serious of issues (which in reality affected only a minority of people), the bread-and-butter issues which faced and threatened large sectors of the public in their everyday life had been relegated to second place.

In many areas 'minor crimes' and incidents of disorder such as street drinking, youths causing annoyance, graffiti, litter and vandalism, accounted for more than half of all calls to the police—over half a million calls annually.

Stories of families' lives being blighted by anti-social tenants, children being bullied, well-tended gardens trashed, and young people unable to walk in their own streets for fear of rival youth, filled local newspapers. Despite our success, were we really matching public expectations?

Public Consultation

During my first nine months as Chief Constable we consulted widely with the public and community representatives at every level to identify their greatest crime concerns. The response was universal, with few surprises. Perhaps for the first time the concerns of the city of Glasgow were being mirrored by those of the rural communities. The public certainly did not want us to lessen our efforts in the investigation of serious crime. What they did want us to do was to give real, co-ordinated attention to the 'minor' quality-of-life crimes which people actually experienced, first hand, on a day-to-day basis. Above all, people wanted to go about their daily business unimpeded by disorderly gangs shouting obscenities, smashing bottles and carrying weapons. They wanted their streets free of litter and graffiti. These were the crimes which the public regarded as most frightening; the crimes that they were most likely to witness or experience firsthand; the crimes that threatened their quality of life. Allied to this, they wanted the reassurance of the 'feel-safe factor' provided by policemen patrolling their streets.

So What had Gone Wrong?

By concentrating primarily on more serious crimes and less on more minor infractions, I believe we had taken our eye off the ball and allowed a problem, perhaps less dramatic than drugs or guns but more insidious and far-reaching, to thrive. The reality was that the 'Glesga' Hard Man' of the 1960s and 1970s had made way for the doped up, spitting yob standing on the street corner, underpass, or local park, drinking 'buckie' (cheap wine) and humiliating passers-by, felt tip pen at the ready to publicly inscribe the current fashionable obscenity. Not a Glasgow-led phenomenon this time, the problem occurred as frequently in Milngavie, Ayr, East Kilbride or Oban, as in the Glasgow 'schemes'. Crimes of disorder transcended all social and geographical barriers.

In common with America, we had undergone a decade of attempting to *understand* and *explain* the behaviour of this loutish minority. 'Understanding' did nothing to stop the problem, and little to alleviate the misery experienced by the law-abiding majority. Reflecting society, we had chosen to follow a path of defining deviancy down, and behaviour that had been unacceptable to previous generations, and dealt with by law enforcement, was neglected. The time was ripe for positive action.

Widespread erosion of parental responsibility had not helped. The era of the parent who chastised their errant child for unruly behaviour or expected their child home at a reasonable hour had diminished, replaced by a 'not my son/daughter' attitude. New police technology and practices had also played their part. The public's demand for a speeded-up police response during the 1970s and 1980s had seen the universal adoption of the fast car, enhanced technology, and the personal radio. Combined, they ensured a less personal police style.

The car, 'the steel box', provided a physical barrier to community interaction. The personal radio, whilst producing a vital step forward in communication which no officer would now forfeit, also gave rise to problems. Officers became increasingly reliant on it to deliver instructions on where to call and what to do. Where, previously, officers' actions were driven by personal initiative, time between calls now seemed in danger of becoming aimless and unfocused. The upshot of the new technology was that officers were increasingly in cars, tied to the radio, waiting for the next call. Officers who attended calls via the radio controller had fulfilled their day's requirements. In short, the radio had surreptitiously provided a minimum service-level agreement for its host officer. A further side-effect of this 'improved service' was that intelligence passed to officers during casual conversation with their community was also lost.

The overriding priority placed on beat officers to answer calls promptly had robbed them of their time-honoured discretion and self-motivation. Whilst the idea of community policing had retained favour in Strathclyde, the balance between providing a 'quality' response or a 'fast' response was arguably weighted in favour of the latter, although it was not always, or indeed generally, the case that one precluded the other.

A Move away from the Operation

My first public statement as Chief Constable included a determination that I would not initiate short-term 'operations'. Whilst they had ameliorated many of the force's problems, and had undoubtedly taken the force forward, the time was right for Strathclyde Police to embark on a longer-term strategy which would embrace the principles of partnership with the community, a concept I felt the 'operation' did not fully explore or exploit.

I held other reservations about the use of 'operations'. They were reactive, their single-issue focus made them inflexible and their short lifespan left little time for lessons to be learned or improvements to be implemented. There was also a heavy reliance on teams of specially selected officers. I have always believed that the most important police officer in the force is the officer on the beat. It is on this officer that the public relies, and it is to support this officer that every other police rôle exists. A major concern over the continued use of short-term operations was that the creation of 'élite', squads composed of what were regarded as the 'best' officers, resulted in a *perceived* downgrading of the status of the beat or community constable. I stress the word 'perceived' because this was never the intention, simply a by-product of the 'operation' syndrome. Abstractions from core shifts left remaining officers feeling undervalued, uninvolved and bearing the work load of their 'élite' colleagues.

A Longer-term Strategy

The long-term strategy I wished to put in place then had to address several key issues: minor crime; public fear of crime; focused, intelligence-led policing in the community; parental responsibility and corporate working. I also demanded the strategy to provide, in a long-term way, the full benefits of the short-term operation and involve every single officer and member of police support staff. As a former detective, I was acutely aware that this all had to be done without ever taking the finger off the pulse in terms of serious crime.

Impossible? No! I believed it could be done. I hold the firm belief that minor and serious crime are not poles apart. Indeed, I believe that minor crime is often simply the breeding ground and nursery that spawns and nurtures more serious and violent crime. Similarly, day-on-day disruption of minor crime creates an environment which is inhospitable to the active criminal. With this in mind, the Spotlight Initiative was born.

The Basics of The Spotlight Initiative

Strathclyde Police was the first force in the United Kingdom to adopt an approach which deliberately set out to tackle minor crime as a priority, on a force-wide basis. By harnessing the full effort of the force, maximising the effect of their presence on the street, making greater use of intelligence and crime management systems, and working corporately with the departments of each of our 12 unitary authorities, and every other group with a legitimate interest in reducing crime, the initiative sought to increase detections, reduce the opportunities to commit crime, demonstrate our commitment to our core task of maintaining law and order and reduce the fear of crime.

A unique concept, the Initiative combines the strengths of the 'operation' with successful components of various other ongoing projects within my own force and other forces, both in this country and abroad, and includes elements of the 'Broken Windows' theory, put forward by Wilson and Kelling.[1]

The result of considerable public and internal consultation, the initiative has four fundamental principles pivotal to its success:

1. It must address public concerns

The police must listen to the public and respond effectively to their concerns.

2. It must fully exploit Corporate Partnerships

Working corporately with local authorities and every other agency or group with a legitimate interest in community safety was and is fundamental to Strathclyde Police achieving its maximum potential. We do not have sole jurisdiction over crime prevention. This has to be viewed as part of an overall commitment to community safety, the promotion of which requires effective and co-ordinated corporate action by every possible sector of the community.

Soon after my appointment, Strathclyde Regional Council was disaggregated as a result of a further reorganisation of local government to form 12 new unitary authorities. Strathclyde Police itself remained a single entity but was now accountable to 12 separate councils, each with different problems and priorities. Liaison was now undertaken via the Strathclyde Joint Police Board, a committee comprising elected representatives from each council, and led by Councillor Bill Timoney, a solid supporter of anti-crime measures, with whom the force had previously enjoyed a productive relationship. Whilst reorganisation meant considerable upheaval for the council, it presented both a challenge and an opportunity for Strathclyde Police.

I viewed the full and mutual exploitation of corporate working as a mainstay of the Spotlight Initiative. In this area, perhaps above all others, lay the realisation of my hopes for a safer environment for the people of Strathclyde.

This area also demanded the adoption of a realistic approach. Not all councils had the same priorities, or the availability of funding and resources. It was a huge challenge, and not without its difficulties, but one where the potential rewards in terms of improving the quality of life for the public were immense.

An agenda was presented by Divisional Commanders to each Local Authority, (the 15 Divisions of Strathclyde police loosely correspond with the boundaries of the 12 new unitary authorities) seeking, amongst other things, improved environmental 'clean-up' resources—graffiti removal, litter uplift and vandalism repairs—and an increase in the provision of diversion facilities for the young.

The issue of clean-up is one in which I fully concur with the 'Broken Windows' theory and a trip round certain areas of my force confirmed this as an issue which merited attention. Untended graffiti, vandalism, litter and broken bottles strewn in public areas were frequently in evidence, particularly in under-passes which were designed to increase public safety. The visible evidence of these acts undoubtedly increased the perception and fear of crime. Incidents often went unreported, and consequently unrepaired, leading to further acts of destruction which added to an impression of neglect. Of particular concern was broken bottle debris which could easily be used as weapons.

On the issue of youth diversion, it is often the practice that police undertake this role. However worthwhile, it removes officers from their core duties of 'guard, watch and patrol', the rôle we had already identified as being what the public expected from us. Diversion is rightly an issue which the police should support and encourage, but it should not be their function. For example, the police should visit the youth disco or fledgling football team to ensure that they are not undermined by the intrusion and actions of thugs.

3. **It must address Serious Crime through Concentration on Minor Crime**

Based on the acceptance that minor crime is not a separate entity from serious crime, and that the two are in fact inextricably linked, the initiative aimed to reduce serious and in particular violent crime through identifying and tackling minor issues.

4. **There Must be Maximum Presence of Officers on the Beat**

There must be a firm commitment to maximising officer presence on the street, with the dual intention of providing reassurance to the public, thus reducing fear of crime and—a threat to the criminal—increasing fear of detection. Patrol time would now be more focused, targeted, intelligence-led and highly visible, to ensure maximum presence in core areas at core times, with the emphasis firmly on community policing. Specialist teams would not be created. Spotlight-style policing was to be the daily function of every available officer.

In order to increase presence on the street, I committed my force to using 'extraordinary' measures. Additional funding was not anticipated, therefore other ways had to be found within the existing budget. During the initial three month period, all non-urgent training was suspended, and officers employed in training and administration duties both at divisions and headquarters were detailed street or public transport patrols in support of divisions. Through prudent control of other budgets, some funding was diverted towards overtime, to be used strictly for the purpose of Spotlight. Special Constables—volunteers who patrol with the regular force—were given full public order training and encouraged to increase attendance for duty at the most strategic times. In addition, all officers were to wear reflective yellow jackets whilst on patrol to ensure that their presence on the street was seen—not only by the public but by the criminal.

Spotlight was not covert policing, but rather a demonstration that the police were present and in great strength.

Whilst formal, non-essential training was suspended, training itself was far from abandoned. Training staff were given the task of compiling training and good practice packages to be delivered locally to all officers before they tackled each Spotlight. Refresher training on police powers and old and new legislation were given to every officer along with useful guidance and tactics. This reinforcement of grass-roots training instilled a new confidence in officers.

Shift sergeants were reminded of briefing skills and video presentations were made to every officer to ensure that they were fully aware of the goals of the initiative. No specialist squads were taken from the shifts. The very existence of already created plain clothes units had to be justified, and every shift and community officer left shift briefings with a feeling that he or she had an important task. Every force resource from Traffic Department, to Mounted Branch, from headquarters administration departments to Surveillance and Drug Squads, was to be used to support the officer on the street. It is my opinion that an officer who is well trained, properly briefed and directed, and who feels that he or she acts with the support of the public is a formidable agent of change.

The Practice of Spotlight

During the initial three months the force focused on eleven 'areas' highlighted by the public as being of greatest concern. Some topics were crime specific, whilst others were location specific:

Carrying of weapons	Vandalism	Truancy
Underage drinking	Drinking in public	Sporting events
Street robberies	Parks and public places	Litter & public
Transport network	Licensed premises	nuisance

The inclusion of one further Spotlight which we called 'Hot Spots' allowed each of the 15 Divisional Commanders within the force area to concentrate on their most pressing local concerns, with the benefit of additional resourcing provided from the centre.

A Consultancy Unit comprising a team of eight officers of varying ranks and service was seconded to work from police headquarters to support the divisional response. Each brought expertise in a range of fields. A Superintendent with broad uniform and detective experience, a Detective Inspector with detailed knowledge of criminal intelligence, a Sergeant with previous marketing experience, a Chief Inspector from community policing, a Constable skilled in local authority liaison, an Administration Constable, a young beat officer to ensure that the first hand views of the officer on the street were heard, and an Inspector who had formerly worked in the Force Media Relations Section made up the team. Overseen by Mr Peter Gibson, my Assistant Chief Constable (Operations), their role was to inform, support, co-ordinate, advise and communicate with each of the 15 commanders responsible for the 15 divisions of the force. It was not the role of the Unit to direct or instruct as it was imperative to Spotlight's success that responsibility for driving the initiative lay locally. Autonomy, ownership and ultimately accountability lay with each commander.

The 'Spotlight' Tactic—The 'Operation' Ingredient

Over the three month intensive introductory phase of the campaign each of the 12 topics were tackled at different times. The term Spotlight, referred to the fact that during a particular, strategic wedge of time, ranging from a few hours to a few days, the attention of every available officer in the force would be directed towards dealing with that single topic. On occasion, a particular Spotlight was revisited several times whilst others were dealt with only once. The Spotlight tactic itself provided all the benefits of the short-term operation in a sustainable long-term way. A strong, heavily publicised attack on a particular crime over a short period of time ensured that the criminal and the public were aware of police activity whilst the long-term commitment ensured that the criminal knew also that police activity would not stop at the end of three months. This time the pressure would not let up and the criminal could not return to *status quo* when the operation ended. Such bursts of police activity were manpower intensive for a short time only, and therefore sustainable indefinitely. The criminal would always have to be on guard!

Many Spotlights, such as sporting events, had to be planned well in advance whilst others were staged on a lightning basis, in response to particular circumstances. For example, a weapons Spotlight was sprung at short notice as a swift response to a previous weekend of violence. By using short bursts of activity, in often innovative ways, combined with widespread publicity and the firm promise that we would revisit that crime again, I planned that a long-term effect on crime would be achieved. By creating an awareness of police actions through the media, I believed that the criminal would be deterred and the public reassured. I also anticipated that the minor crimes dealt with would uncover more serious crimes. To date, the signs are encouraging.

The Achievements ... So Far

Our first Spotlight encompassed all 12 topics, targeting suspects who had failed to submit themselves to court for trial and for whom judicial warrants had been issued. On the day Spotlight was launched almost 400 men and women were arrested in dawn raids, relaying the clear message to the criminal that we meant business. The longer-term effect is that our courts are now finding fewer people failing to attend, fewer warrants are being issued, and consequently less police time is being spent tracking offenders.

Tackling knives and weapons—a major focus of the initiative—saw 43,000 people searched and the proportion of those found carrying weapons almost halved over the three months. 'Carrying of knives' crimes fell by 40 per cent on the corresponding three months of the previous year and early indications are that many hospitals treated fewer casualties of weapon violence. For the first time violent crime fell, by 3.8 per cent—not dramatic by any standards, but significant nonetheless.

Following truancy Spotlights during which we worked closely with local authority attendance officers to successfully trace and return 1,000 pupils to school over four days, several schools in the area reported their lowest level of truancy since statistics were collated.

A single Spotlight lasting only six hours which homed in on drinking alcohol in public places—a major source of public annoyance—built on good work already being done, and saw the problem all but disappear, to the extent that this exercise has not had to be repeated. A total of 300 people were reported to the Procurator Fiscal but hundreds more were simply warned at the discretion of the individual officer, and asked to discard their alcohol.

Licensees were targeted heavily, a 400 per cent increase in prosecutions for selling alcohol to children being recorded, but of equal significance, a relationship was established with the various licensed trade associations supportive of encouraging responsible behaviour among their members.

Over the three month period, detections for those crimes which we directly sought to target—disorder, petty assault, public drinking and public nuisance offences—rose by 30 per cent. Other serious crimes, which we hoped to indirectly affect, were also influenced. Car crime fell by 22 per cent; housebreaking by 13 per cent; vandalism by seven per cent. Through the direct targeting of minor offences, more drugs were recovered than ever before. Whilst targeting litter, transport and truancy, firearms including loaded handguns and other potentially lethal, criminally held weapons were recovered prior to causing injury. An excellent and productive relationship was struck with our colleagues, British Transport Police, providing mutual aid and increasing police presence on public transport in the Strathclyde area. This saw crime on the rail network fall by 20 per cent, making it one of the safest in the country.

Serious crime excluding drugs (seizures of which rose as a result of increased police activity in relation to stop-and-search procedures and improved intelligence) fell by 9.6 per cent whilst its detection rate rose by four per cent.

Whilst encouraging, these statistics alone paint a hollow picture, and are not the benchmark on which this initiative should be deemed a success or otherwise.

From the outset, I said that the Spotlight Initiative was to be a long-term strategy. Its philosophy was to change our way of working and our approach to dealing with crime. No longer would we deal with crime in isolation, but rather, we would seek meaningful partnerships with other agencies to increase the likelihood of effecting a long-term solution. Our approach must be both traditional and innovative using random beat patrol and intelligent targeting. Besides putting our own policing strategies in place, the initial three month phase of Spotlight was intended to develop structures and relationships with other partners which would complement police activity and lead to increased benefits for the community. In terms of corporate working, we could not be certain at the outset what we would achieve. What was clear was that it could not happen overnight.

The achievements during the first three months were above our expectations. Liaison between each Division and their respective Authority occurred at all levels, from practitioner (constable and sergeant/council service provider e.g. joiner, street sweeper, teacher) to middle management (police inspector and superintendent/council foremen and heads of departments) and senior management (chief officer and divisional commander/chief executive and elected representatives). All 12 Councils backed the initiative in principle and in action, with the police commitment to community safety reflecting the same priorities as the Councils.

Almost every section of local authority service provision worked with police both on individual operations, and to develop further initiatives, often falling outside the scope of the original Spotlight topics, but with Spotlight as the catalyst.

Existing relationships were firmly consolidated. Council joiners worked alongside officers to expedite door repairs following our warrants operation, minimising time spent by officers protecting unsecured properties. Police protected housing officials carrying out evictions of anti-social tenants engaged in drugs activities, on one occasion unearthing £300,000 worth of heroin destined for the streets of Glasgow. Trading Standards Officials, with enhanced powers of enforcement, worked alongside police prior to 'Guy Fawkes' to ensure fireworks were not sold to children. Social services departments who administrate community service orders directed their offenders to carry out public works including graffiti removal and environmental clean-ups of schools, underpasses, public halls and walkways; schools participated in anti-litter awareness projects; dog fouling bye-law legislation was enacted by many councils with 'pooper scoopers' for the clean up of excrement being provided free of charge to dog owners; school attendance officers patrolled with police; park attendants did likewise. Forums were set up to discuss corporate action to resolve community problems; bureaucracy in some areas was cut, with often dramatic results. One progressive council slashed its repair time for damaged school properties from an average of 11 weeks to the same day. No department has been left untouched and no offer of assistance turned away.

Other agencies have come on board too—from Strathclyde's major 'bus groups, taxi owners' associations and Transport Authority, to the licensed trade associations, local and national media, customs and excise officials, the Department of Social Security, the local Air Training Corps, and even 1,500 milkmen from a major dairy. All played a part. One single corporate operation involving police, Customs and Excise and officials netted over £4 million worth of counterfeit goods, recovered duties and fraudulent benefits.

We also set out to achieve a public 'feel-safe' factor, reducing the fear of crime and thus improving, in some way, the quality of life of many people. Such fear is the product of long-term reinforcement and will not disappear overnight. It is also an issue over which we do not have substantial control. Increasingly sensationalist media coverage, even fictional dramas featuring crime, can affect people's perception of crime, but we must do what we can to ensure that the public is aware of the reality of crime, not the myth. To this end, for the first time, Strathclyde Police allocated the sum of £60,000 to finance a public information campaign—a small sum in advertising terms, but one which bought almost £200,000 worth of advertising space as a result of the goodwill of private companies. It is encouraging to note that an independent survey commissioned by us only six weeks into the initiative identified a small, but significant decrease in the level of fear of crime in the Strathclyde area. This 'feel-safe' factor is the primary measure against which I would seek the initiative be judged—but not yet. There is still much to be done. To date, significant numbers of calls and letters of appreciation have been received from the public supporting the initiative and telling us that they now feel safer as a result.

Public support for the Spotlight Initiative may also be reflected in figures for complaints against the police. Despite greatly increased street activity, including the use of stop-and-search powers, complaints fell by 20 per cent during October to December 1996 compared to the same quarter in 1995—the lowest figures ever recorded.

If people now feel more confident in walking their dog at night, visiting the park, or travelling on public transport, and are able to take pride in their environment without being made to feel that they are the minority, then this is the rod with which I would choose to measure any success. This is the true evaluation of Spotlight.

The Future

Spotlight is here to stay. The community wants it. Our local councils want it. My officers want it. The best of the Spotlight Initiative will now be driven forward with the implementation of lessons learned and the development of the relationships which have been formed. Supervisors have learned to make more efficient and creative use of resources, and to lean towards natural partners to increase their effectiveness.

The initial Spotlight topics remain valid, and will continue to be implemented on a force-wide basis, augmented between times by 'Torchlights'—mini divisional operations which are already proving highly successful. In one particular area, a shopping mall plagued by disruptive youths and drug dealers was targeted numerous times over a month, with all available local officers 'sweeping' through it several times a day, for only a few minutes. A small number of arrests were made and minor offenders warned. The effect of the unpredictable police presence has made it no longer a 'cool' gathering place for hooligans and shoppers have returned. A similar project carried out for ten minute periods over several days on a troublesome bus route had the same effect. Disorder disappeared, it took few resources and the public was reassured. In the same vein, where a serious problem occurs demanding a major response, the force is geared up to provide a swift response, mobilising hundreds of extra officers if necessary in a 'Floodlight' operation.

Plans are also in hand to broaden the scope of Spotlights to include any matter causing public concern, especially those which induce a fear of crime. Handling stolen property, bogus workmen and fraudsters may all come under the Spotlight in the future, with a variety of partners being sought. We have come a long way, but we have further to go. Our infant has yet to mature.

A Divisional Commander in my force renowned for his apt observations anecdotally likened Spotlight to the building trade. 'A builder, asked by a passer-by what he was doing, answered:

"I'm laying bricks, one on top of the other". Another builder when asked the same question responded, "I'm building a cathedral".' Achieving my force objective of Safer Streets is dependent on the actions of motivated officers working towards a shared goal in a highly focused way, supported by the resources of local councils, and the community as a whole. We are not laying bricks. We are building a cathedral.

Notes

Editor's Introduction

1 Dennis, N. and Erdos, G., *Families Without Fatherhood*, London: IEA Health and Welfare Unit, 1992, pp. 89-90.

2 Frank Nix was awarded the Edward Medal—a medal later revoked to become the George Cross. Fortunately *The Times* carried his obituary (he died 8 August 1996), and therefore leaves on public record an exemplary working-class life, what is today called a 'role model'. The details typify the different way in which young men handled their problems of poverty and unemployment in his community as contrasted with the way in which vandals and the like were handling theirs on their estates in the 1990s. 'He ... as a young man in the days of the Depression ... had often taken part in the miners' ride from Tibshelf to Skegness and back, a round trip of 130 miles.'

3 Combe, V., 'Carey is Against Quick-fix Solutions', *Daily Telegraph*, 8 January 1997.

4 By 1997 a main leader writer of the newspaper of the conservative establishment was provoked beyond measure by a New Year message from five bishops to denounce the Church of England (once 'the Tory party at prayer') as a sociology department at prayer. 'If it has ever mentioned the national crime rate ... it is only to blame poverty ... [Yet] one of the principal causes of ... poverty ... is precisely the immoral conduct which they have so signally condoned by failing to condemn.' 'A Shower of Bishops', *Sunday Telegraph*, 5 January 1997.

5 'So far police have arrested and charged 19 adults and juveniles ... All are from the Kendray estate, Barnsley, known locally as the Bronx ... The house had been left empty after the tenant had a row with a neighbour and walked out. Council workmen sealed the door and boarded up the windows ... When it was checked four days later all the contents had been stolen.' The items looted included a two-piece suite, tables, chairs, the TV set, the cooker, a karaoke machine and other electrical equipment. Wilkinson, P., 'Women Stripped House of Contents', *The Times*, 14 December 1996.

6 Pilgrim Trust, *Men Without Work*, with an Introduction by the Archbishop of York, Cambridge: Cambridge University Press, 1938, p. 75.

7 'Ruthless Raver in a Class of Her Own', *The Sunday Times*, 5 January 1997. [Emphasis added.]

8 Through an article in *The Sunday Times Magazine* in November 1989, an expanded version of which was published as *The Emerging British Underclass*, London: IEA Health and Welfare Unit, 1990. The reaction of the social-affairs academic establishment was a chorus of assurances that there was nothing to be alarmed about. He wrote two more articles for *The Sunday Times*, published in May 1994, and reprinted as *Underclass: The Crisis Deepens*, London: IEA Health and Welfare Unit, 1994, by which time both the cogency of his message and the obvious facts all around had muted the opposition somewhat. His series of articles which began with 'Sentenced to a Crime Wave', *The Sunday Times*, 5 January 1997, were hardly challenged on the facts, except by a small and desperate hard core of what Claude Rains called 'the usual suspects'. Charles Murray had already described the American situation as it had developed up to 1980 in his influential book, *Losing Ground: American Social Policy 1950-1980*, New York: Basic Books, 1984.

9 *The British Crime Survey 1996*, London: Home Office, September 1996. This is not the full report. The full report is published later by HMSO.

10 Though this idea is greeted with puzzled amazement, as if it were the greatest novelty in the world, by 'social experts' in the 1990s, right or wrong it is a historical commonplace. Plato's friend Archytas of Tarentum, for example, said in the middle of the fourth century B.C. that sensual greed, 'the most fatal curse given by nature to mankind', incited men to betray their country (no news to the KGB or the CIA), and commit rape, adultery and every other kind of sexual outrage. 'Where [sexual] self-indulgence reigns, decent behaviour is excluded.' Archytas's observation received Cicero's approval in his discourse on old age. Cicero, *Selected Works*, Harmondsworth: Penguin, 1971 pp 228-29.

11 Taken by itself the environmental argument would justify a massive increase in the part of the individual's external circumstances constituted by the police. An additional assumption is therefore necessary and is added, but rarely if ever made explicit—that these 'external circumstances' to which the criminal is powerlessly subject do not include policing itself.

12 Morgan, P., *Delinquent Phantasies*, London: Temple Smith, 1978, p. 57.

13 Murray, C., 'Loading the Scales of Justice', *The Sunday Times*, 19 January 1997.

14 *The Sunday Times*, 11 July 1993.

15 These ideas are propagated in many forms, but most explicitly by the so-called 'post-modernists'. One popular source of post-modernism and deconstructionism has been the writings of the French philosopher Michel Foucault. (See, e.g. his *Madness and Civilization* (1961), London: 1971; *The Order of Things* (1966), London: 1970.)

16 In so far as the report was accurate, the attack was intended to denigrate the Victorians, and by comparison to put modern society in a favourable light. It is the attack on 'Victorian values', which are denigrated today as present in modern society, that is relevant here. *The Sunday Times*, 22 December 1996.

17 'A political organization with continuous operations [*ein politischer Anstaltsbetrieb*] will be called a "state" in so far as its administrative staff successfully upholds the claim to a *monopoly* of the *legitimate* use of physical compulsion in the enforcement of its order.' Weber, M., *Economy and Society: An Outline of Interpretative Sociology*, Berkeley, California: University of California Press, 1978, p. 54.

18 Clutterbuck, C., *Britain in Agony: The Growth of Political Violence*, Harmondsworth: Penguin, 1980. The starkest expression of this weakening of the legitimacy of the state's monopoly of violence is the frequency with which purportedly 'confrontational' interviewers (with reputations for fearless questioning of politicians to protect) fail to challenge terrorists when they put their own use of force in attacking the state on the same footing as the state's use of force in combatting them. 'We want all weapons to be removed!'

19 Hamilton, A., Jay, J. and Madison, J., *The Federalist: A Commentary on the Constitution of the United States* (1792), New York: Random House, 1937.

20 Parsons, T., 'Deviant Behaviour and the Mechanisms of Social Control', *The Social System*, London: Tavistock, 1952, pp. 249-325. Parsons, T. and Bales, R.F., 'Family Structure and the Socialization of the Child', *Family, Socialization and Interaction Process*, London: Routledge and Kegan Paul, 1956.

21 Dewey, J., *Experience and Education* (1938), New York: Macmillan, 1950, p. 13. This was the book's twelfth reprint.

22 *Ibid.*, p. 68.

23 Dewey's explicit advocacy of teaching as surreptitious manipulation rather than open education had aroused feelings of distaste in some quarters much earlier. 'Everything must be straightforward ... and all manipulation avoided by which ingenious pedagogues seek to work upon the characters of their pupils without their knowledge.' Adams, J. (ed.), *The New Teaching*, London: Hodder and Stoughton, 1918, p. 11.

24 Mailer, N., 'The White Negro', in his *Advertisements for Myself*, New York: Putman, 1959.

25 Glazer, N., 'On Subway Graffiti in New York', *The Public Interest*, Winter 1979.

26 Mailer, *op. cit.*, pp. 313, 320-21.

27 Laing, R.D., *The Politics of Experience*, New York: Pantheon, 1967. For a fuller discussion of these developments, see Magnet, M., *The Dream and the Reality: The Sixties' Legacy to the Underclass*, New York: Morrow, 1993.

28 Jack Kerouac's *On the Road* can be taken as the starting point of the widening in the popularity this literature of—a slogan of the 1960s—'turn on, tune in and drop out'.

29 This was certainly true after the impeachment in 1787 of Warren Hastings over his rule as first governor-general of India. In his impeachment speech Burke encapsulated the policy that was to characterize British imperialism and make it distinctive as compared with the imperialism of the other European powers—that Britain should govern other nations 'upon their own principles and not ours'. (Ireland was nearly

always an exceptional case.) When, after the Second World War, the colonial authorities were faced with—say—the Mau Mau in Kenya instead of Gandhi's civil disobedience in India, the 'illegitimacy' of the use of force in the interests of imperialism fed back to some extent to support critical assessments of domestic policing.

30 Howard, M., 'What a Criminal Fears is What Stops Him', *The Sunday Times*, 19 January 1997. Michael Howard wrote this article as the current Home Secretary.

31 In the United States there was a five-fold increase in violent crime from the mid-1950s to the mid-1990s. With every decade teenage violence in particular became not only more frequent, but also nastier. Between 1990 and 1994 there were 120,000 murders—twice the death toll of the Vietnam War. All this was during a period of economic prosperity when there had been no depression resembling the scale of that of the early 1930s, and there had been a five-fold increase in social expenditure in real terms. See Bennett, W.J., Dilulio, J.J. Jr. and Walters, J.P., *Moral Poverty and How to Win America's War Against Crime and Drugs*, New York: Simon and Schuster, 1996.

32 See, for example, Kelling, G.L. and Coles, C.M., *Broken Windows: Restoring Order and Reducing Crime in Our Communities*, New York: Free Press, 1996. This is an assessment of the new crime-reduction policing policies in New York City (especially in the subways), Seattle, Buffalo and San Francisco.

Crime is Down in New York City: Blame the Police

1 The US equivalent of the 999 emergency services telephone number.

2 Wilson, J.Q. and Kelling, G.L., 'Broken Windows', *Atlantic Monthly*, March 1982, pp. 29-38.

3 Harvard Business School Case Study #N9-396-293, 11 April 1996, pp.8-9.

Zero Tolerance: Short-term Fix, Long-term Liability?

1 Wilson, J.Q. and Kelling, G.L., 'Broken Windows', *Atlantic Monthly*, March 1982, pp. 29-38.

2 *Ibid.*, p. 30.

3 Goldstein, H., *Problem Oriented Policing*, London: McGraw Hill, 1991.

4 The full 'aim' of the Thames Valley Police is:

'Working with our communities, to reduce crime, disorder and fear, as the leading caring and professional Police Service'.

'The Thames Valley "STYLE" of policing is characterised by:
• consultation with local communities
• working in partnership with other agencies
• tackling causes, not just symptoms.

We call this Problem-Solving Policing.'

5 Government White Paper on Police Reform, London: HMSO, 1993, para. 2.2.

6 Perhaps the most appropriate example is the Brixton disorders on 10-12 April 1981. In his report the Rt. Hon. the Lord Scarman, OBE criticised the style of policing operated in Brixton—including inflexibility, overreaction to minor disorder, and 'saturation' patrolling of the streets. Lord Scarman named the policing of Brixton as one of the factors which contributed to the disorders. 'Report to the Rt. Hon. William Whitelaw CH, MC, MP, Secretary of State for the Home Department, on the Brixton Disorders of 10-12 April 1981', London: HMSO, November 1981.

7 In 1994 there were 1,561 recorded murders and non-negligent manslaughters in New York City; there were 167 in London. Source: *Crime in the United States 1995*, US Department of Justice, and *Criminal Statistics England & Wales 1995*, Home Office.

8 *Ibid.* In 1994 there were 2,667 reported rapes, and 72,588 reported robberies, in New York City; there were 1,375 reported rapes and 25,793 reported robberies in London.

9 In October 1995 there were 37,449 sworn officers in the NYPD, serving a population of 7,319,546. In the Metropolitan Police there were 28,042 police officers serving a population of 7,106,935. Thames Valley Police, with 3,778 police officers, serve a population of 2,014,148. Sources: NYPD; *Crime in the United States 1995*; Home Office; Thames Valley Police.

10 'Setting the Standards for Policing: Meeting Community Expectations', ACPO Strategic Policy Document, *Operational Policing Review*, February 1990.

11 Audit Commission, *Streetwise: Effective Police Patrol*, London: HMSO, 1996.

Confident Policing in Hartlepool

1 Sources of information in Hartlepool were unfailingly helpful, from the *Hartlepool Mail*, the librarians and officials of all kinds, to pleasant couples just passing by on estates or people at market stalls, who politely wanted to know how they could assist a man strangely making notes, and were eager to contribute their own knowledge of crime and policing in their home town. Without detracting from the value of all their contributions, we should like to thank Principal Planning Officer Richard Waldmeyer by name for sharing his knowledge with us.

2 Gun incidents in Hartlepool from August 1994 to March 1996:-
August 1994: Scrap dealer Terry Richardson is shot through a window at his West View home.
August 1995: Graham Read's home on the Owton Manor estate is shot at.
October 1995: Brian Kerr is shot as he tries to flee from a gang who burst into his home.
February 1996: Harry Lancaster is thought to have turned a gun on himself after shooting his father in his home on the Owton Manor estate.
March 1996: Armed police called to the Middleton Grange shopping centre after a man is spotted with a pistol.
March 1996: Graham Read is involved in a second shooting incident.
Source: Hunter, N., 'Get These Guns Off Our Streets', *Hartlepool Mail*, 26 March 1996.

3 *Cleveland Constabulary: Chief Inspector's Annual Report 1994-95*, p. 20.

4 *Hartlepool Mail*, 11 November 1995. The Court of Appeal did increase his sentence (*Hartlepool Mail*, 5 March 1996).

5 Shaw, B., *Cleveland Constabulary: Chief Inspector's Annual Report 1995-1996*, p. 5.

6 Bone, J., 'New York Curbs Its Murder Rate', *The Times*, 30 December 1996. Murray, C., 'Loading the Scales of Justice', *The Sunday Times*, 19 January 1997; and Letts, Q., 'Joining the Resistance in the Big Apple', *The Times*, 24 January 1997.

7 'Yearly Statistics for Hartlepool', supplied by Hartlepool District of Cleveland Constabulary.

8 There were 2,300 thefts of vehicles in 1994, down to 1,000 in 1996.
   In 1994 the average monthly figure for thefts of vehicles was 192. In 1996 the average monthly figure was 84.
   In 1994 the lowest monthly figure was 134. In 1996 the lowest monthly figure was 56. *Ibid.*

9 There were 2,700 domestic burglaries in 1994, down to 1,900 in 1996.
   In 1994 the average monthly figure for domestic burglaries was 225. In 1996 the average monthly figure as 155.
   In 1994 the lowest monthly figure was 161. In 1996 the lowest monthly figure was 89. *Ibid.*

10 There were 2,200 thefts from vehicles in 1994, down to 1,800 in 1996.
   In 1994 the average monthly figure for thefts from vehicles was 180. In 1996 the average monthly figure was 153.
   In 1994 the lowest monthly figure was 110. In 1996 the lowest monthly figure was 101. *Ibid.*

11 *Chief Inspector's Report 1995-1996*, p. 5.

12 *Hartlepool Mail*, 1 August 1996.

13 *Criminal Statistics England and Wales*, London: HMSO, annually.

14 *Evening Gazette* (Teesside), 19 December 1996.

15 *Ibid.*

16 Dennis, N. and Erdos, G., *Families Without Fatherhood*, London: IEA Health and Welfare Unit, 1993, p. xv.

17 *Chief Constable's Report 1995-1996*, p. 4.

18 Murray, C., *The Sunday Times*, 19 January 1997.

19 Howard, M., *The Sunday Times*, 9 January 1997.

20 Ray Mallon's comment, reported in: Hunter, N., 'Crime in Town Hits a New Low as Police Get Tough', *Hartlepool Mail*, 7 July 1996.

21 Steele, J., 'My Beat Has Become Boring, Says the Police Chief Who Cut Crime', *Daily Telegraph*, 21 January 1997.

22 *Ibid.*

23 *Chief Constable's Report 1995-1996*, p. 4.

24 McCormack, M.H., *The 110% Solution*, London: Chapman, 1990. (Pan Books, 1992.)

25 *Chief Constable's Report 1995-1996*, p. 4.

26 *Hartlepool Mail*, 10 July 1996.

27 Jesney, J., 'Detective Ray Talks to Nation on Tough Stance', *Hartlepool Mail*, 1 August 1996.

28 *Hartlepool Mail*, 22 April 1996.

29 *Hartlepool Mail*, 10 July 1996.

30 *Hartlepool Mail*, 6 July 1996.

31 Howard, M., *The Sunday Times*, 19 January 1997. Michael Howard was writing as Home Secretary.

32 *Hartlepool Mail*, 15-19 May 1995.

33 *Hartlepool Mail*, 15-19 May 1995.

34 Hunter, N., 'Out of Touch', *Hartlepool Mail*, 15 November 1995.

35 He addressed, for example, a meeting in Hull attended by 500 members of the Humberside Association of Neighbourhood Watch Groups.

36 *Hartlepool Mail*, 3 April 1996.

37 He adds, 'but it was not in that spirit that they fought'. Orwell, G., 'England Your England' [from *The Lion and the Unicorn* (1941)], *The Orwell Reader*, New York: Harcourt, Brace, 1956, p. 253.

38 Jesney, A., 'Teesside Post for Popular Detective', *Hartlepool Mail*, 9 September 1996.

39 Jesney, A., 'The Strong Arm of the Law', *Hartlepool Mail*, 9 August 1996.

40 Jesney, A., 'No Let-up in the Fight Against Criminals: Acting DCI to Keep up the Good Work', *Hartlepool Mail*, 13 August 1996.

Crime and Culture in Hartlepool

1 Bogdanor, V. and Skidelsky, R. (eds.), *The Age of Affluence 1951-1964*, London: Macmillan, 1970.

2 Sayers, R.S., *A History of Economic Change in England 1880-1939*, Oxford: Oxford University Press, 1967, pp. 45-59.

3 *Hartlepool Local Plan*, Borough of Hartlepool, May 1994, p. 14.

4 Truancy and truancy-related crime were being dealt with by a Non-Attenders' Project, involving government funds for computerized school registers and a support unit 'to rehabilitate perpetual non-attenders and disaffected children'.

   Two Detached Youth Workers were to be employed to raise awareness about 'sexual health, drugs and alcohol' among the 16-24 year-olds on the two estates.

   The sports' facilities would be linked in such a way as to enhance 'security and control', with the assistance of 'a comprehensive closed-circuit TV system'.

   The Crime Prevention Panel of one of the local schools promotes 'drug education' and co-operates with the local police in combating 'petty crime'. The Police, Fire and Ambulance service puts on anti-crime displays to the area's primary-school children of, for example, the danger to the culprit's own life and limb of 'joyriding'—of crashing the car taken without the owner's consent.

   A project entitled the Good, the Bad and the Ugly will use a team from Hartlepool Borough Council to lead 'workshops' in the schools of the two housing estates, through which the pupils can voice their opinions on various topics, including crime.

5 *Sunderland City News*, No. 4, January 1997.

6   In 1991 over 99 per cent of Hartlepool's residents were white. Of the less than one in a hundred 'in ethnic groups other than white', more than half were from the Indian sub-continent (an ethnic group that in England performs significantly better in school and at work than the English they live among). A further 15 per cent were Chinese (whose educational and economic performance is even higher than that of the Asians). OPCS, *Census 1991: Key Statistics for Local Authorities*, London: HMSO, 1994, p. 84.

7   The overall figure for Hartlepool was 0.7 per cent. In three of the worst wards the ethnic minority figures were 0.2 per cent, 0.3 per cent, and 0.4 per cent. Cleveland County Joint Strategic Unit Information System, *Area Snapshots*, mimeographed.

8   Martin, R., *Historical Notes and Personal Recollections of West Hartlepool and Its Founder*, West Hartlepool: Martin, 1924, p. 151 and pp. 166-69.

9   *Ibid*, p. 152.

10 Cowley, C., *Air Raids on the Hartlepools: Reprinted from Articles in the* Northern Daily Mail, 1943. No publisher shown. (Photocopy in Hartlepool central library.)

11 Tribute to Ted Leadbitter, MP, Radio Cleveland, 24 December 1996.

12 Many people can remember, and talk about, the films they saw in the 1940s or 1950s at the Empire. Sitting in Macdonald's today, the epitome of the delocalized milieu, they can still easily find themselves chatting to an otherwise complete stranger about the school that (it turns out) they both went to as children, and very easily discover that they have common acquaintances. Hartlepudlians used to arrange to meet one another under the clock of Lamb's the jewellers in Lynn Street. By 1996 even that was back in working order, and pensioners were reminiscing about all the proposals of marriage that had been made under it. The local press knew that there were readers interested in such things, because so many of them had been participants in them.
    'He Had Just Enough Money For Special Ring', *Hartlepool Mail*, 16 December 1996.

13 In 1912 more than 240 ships of the mercantile marine had 'Hartlepool' on their stern.

14 Between 1878 and 1900 the annual output of one of Hartlepool's ship-yards was on six occasions the highest of any in Britain.

15 Hartlepool yards had built 33 ships totalling 178,000 gross tons in 1913. In 1931 they built none, in 1933 they again built none, and in 1935 they built only two, together 10,000 gross tons. Hartlepool imported about two-thirds of the pit-props for the Durham and Midlands coalfield. In 1927 it imported over 0.8 million tones of pit props. By 1933 this figure had been reduced to 0.4 million tons. Fish landing had been 17,000 tons in 1920; in 1933 only 7,000 tons were landed. In 1920 the value of imports had been £5 million. In the early 1930s the value was under £1 million. This was a much more severe loss than either the Tyne or the Humber ports, where the value of imports was reduced in the period by one half. Lock, M., *The Hartlepools: A Survey and Plan*, West Hartlepool: West Hartlepool Borough Council, 1948, p. 41.

16 Lock, *op. cit.*, p. 31.

17 Shipbuilding at Hartlepool ended with the completion of the 'Blanchland' on 31 October 1961. Spaldin, S., *Shipbuilders of the Hartlepools*, Hartlepool: Hartlepool Borough Council, 1986.

18 *Ibid.*, p. 31.

19 See the account of interwar British policing—and of provincial life before the 1914-18 war—given convincingly from his own experience by Harry Daley, a police constable who because of his intelligence and sexual orientation became a minor darling of the Bloomsbury Group. Daley, H., *This Small Cloud*, London: 1986.

20 Sayers, *op. cit.*, p. 94.

21 Lock, *op. cit.*, p. 23.

22 Lock, *op. cit.*

23 The population of England and Wales had risen 1860-1901 from 20 million to 32 million. The number of recorded crimes had fallen from 88,000 to 81,000. *Criminal Statistics England and Wales*, London: HMSO, annually.

24 Lock, *op. cit.*

25 In housing, by the mid-1990s the five basic amenities, including the internal w.c., were universally provided. Only 1.2 per cent of households lacked or shared the use of a bath or shower and/or a w.c. The statistics now dealt rather with 'no car' households (47 per cent) and households without central heating (23 per cent). By the time of the Census of 1991 the category of 'more than 1.5 persons per room' had been discarded as irrelevant to modern housing conditions, and only two per cent of Hartlepool's households lived even at more than *one* person per room. The rent of the poor was paid as housing benefit by the state.

26 *Hartlepool: A Community That's Making It Happen*, Hartlepool City Challenge, no date [1996?].

27 OPCS, *Key Population and Vital Statistics: Local and Health Authority Areas*, London: HMSO, 1993, p. 100. The national figures were 24 per cent males, 25 per cent females.

28 A recent report—not about Hartlepool—shows the extent to which the route to education beyond school has been opened up since the 1950s. An A-level equivalent is now on offer which is accepted for entry to at least one University and to other institutions of further and higher education in which one of the skills required is 'cooking for seduction'. *The Independent*, 7 November 1996.

29 In the worst ward for unemployment, St. Hilda's, only 70 per cent of the economically active males were employed. There were other wards where fewer than 80 per cent of the men had jobs. The town figure is for May, the ward figures are for January. Office for National Statistics and the Tees Valley Joint Strategy Unit.

30 Mill, J.S., 'Of Local Representative Bodies', *On Representative Government*, London: 1861.

31 Membership card PAA 730565, Whitburn and Marsden Club and Institute, 1985.

32 The rules of nearly all working men's clubs closely followed the models laid down by the Working Men's Club and Institute Union. The clubs enjoyed certain privileges over other establishments selling alcoholic drinks by having their rules registered under the current Industrial and Provident Society Acts.

33 *Hartlepool: A Community That's Making It Happen*, Hartlepool City Challenge, no date [1996?].

34 The words are those of Samuel Smiles, in a passage in which he tries to account for the extraordinary fortitude that the British civilians besieged in Lucknow showed during the Indian Mutiny. The passage is particularly apt when applied to Hartlepool, for the remembered 'hero of Lucknow' was a north-easterner, General Havelock, whose statue stands in Trafalgar Square, and whose name used to grace many a north-east pub and at least one cinema. It is doubly apt, because in his *Autobiography* Smiles writes that *Self-Help* was written to illustrate and enforce the power of another north-easterner's 'great word'—Perseverance. Smiles, S., *Self-Help: With Illustrations of Conduct and Perseverance* (1859), London: IEA Health and Welfare Unit, 1996, pp. 143-44. Although the book is called *Self-Help* it is quite clear that it could have been with equal propriety called *Mutual Improvement*, for it emphasizes so much the importance of self-striving and self-improving people working with and for one another.

35 Sacks, J., 'Faith in the Family: Devaluing Domesticity is Fatal to Society', *The Times*, 25 February 1997.

36 Moser, C.A. and Scott, W., *British Towns: A Statistical Study of their Social and Economic Differences*, Edinburgh: Oliver and Boyd, 1961, p. 116.

37 About 45 per cent of the children born outside marriage were registered by cohabiting couples.

38 The highest rate of children born outside marriage was in one of the poorest and in parts most ravaged urban areas of England, Knowsley, Merseyside (just under 50 per cent). The lowest rate was in Richmondshire, North Yorkshire (12.5 per cent). OPCS, *Key Population and Vital Statistics: Local and Health Authority Areas*, London: HMSO, 1993.

By the mid-1990s the middle- and upper-classes had bought in on an enormous scale a new set of domestic employees to act *in loco parentis*, as a sort of second family for their children. (See *The Sunday Times*, 5 January 1997.)

39 'Clare Rayner, the agony aunt, said ... "Sexual probity is a luxury. You have to have a roof over your head and a job to afford a wife and children."' Daniels, A., 'Crime "due to lax morality"', *Guardian*, 2 January 1997.

40 Mason, P., *The English Gentleman: The Rise and Fall of and Ideal* (1982), London: Pimlico, 1993, p. 214. The vast area of the Sudan (four times the area of Texas) was ruled with a high degree of consent by a corps of administrators (the Sudan Political Service) that in the fifty-six years of its existence never exceeded 400 British officials, and rarely exceeded more than 120. Dame Margery Perham wrote that the colonial District Commissioner was one of the 'supreme types' produced by British culture. Perham, M., 'Introduction' to Henderson, K.D.D., *The Making of Modern Sudan*, London: 1953, p. xiii.

41 Gorer, G.E.S., *Exploring English Character*, London: Cresset Press, 1955.

42 Letter of 28 September 1984. Harrison, T., *The Durham Phenomenon*, London: Darton, Longman and Todd, 1985, pp. 104-05.

Strathclyde's Spotlight Initiative

1   Wilson, J.Q. and Kelling, G.L., 'Broken Windows', *Atlantic Monthly*, March 1982, pp. 29-38.